SECOND CHANCE

The Inspiring Story of One Woman's Fight for Life

DIANE HÉBERT

LESTER
&ORPEN
DENNYS
PUBLISHERS

FIRST EDITION

The Publisher wishes to thank the Canada Council for its support in the translation of this book.

Canadian Cataloguing in Publication Data

Hébert, Diane
    Second chance

Translation of: Un second souffle
ISBN   0-88619-222-6

1. Hébert, Diane.   2. Heart - Transplantation - Patients - Quebec (Province) - Biography.
3. Lungs - Transplantation - Patients - Quebec (Province) - Biography.   I.   Fontaine, Rachel, 1946-   . II. Title.

RD598.H4214   1988   362.1'97412   C88-94010-7

Unless otherwise indicated, photographs are from Diane Hébert's personal album; most were taken by Yves Kochenburger.

Printed and bound in Canada

Lester & Orpen Dennys Limited
78 Sullivan Street
Toronto, Canada   M5T 1C1

For my two loves,
       Isabelle and Yves

And for you whom I do not know
but who passed on your life to me,
my deepest thanks to you and your family
for this gift of love.
I will carry you always in my heart.

Contents

Acknowledgements

I wish to express my warmest thanks to the following people who gave me their support throughout this long ordeal:

My mother, Cécile; my father, Robert; my sister, Claudette, her husband and their children, as well as my whole family; Sylvie, François, Fernande and Yves Kochenburger, Hélène Gravel and Jean Kochenburger, Maître Daniel Kochenburger;

Charlotte Byrne of Château d'Aujourd'hui, Chuck Walter, Huguette and Jimmy Dewavrin, Dorothy and Kenneth Pelphrey, Claudette and Jean-Paul Théorêt, Gaétane Bergman, Christiane Catin, Monsieur et Madame Savoie, Simone and Jean-Claude Durantet;

Dr. Marc Frenette, Suzanne Cabana-Martel, Yvon Royal, all the members of the Laval Optimist Club, especially Dr. Michel Dallaire, Pierre Francoeur, Guy Crevier, Raymond Lussier, and Jean-François Martel;

Dr. Joel Cooper and his team at Toronto General Hospital, the staff of Intensive Care South, and of the tenth and eleventh floors of the Norman Urquhart Wing;

Air Canada, Caisses Populaires Desjardins, André Montmorency, the Laval Police Department, and journalists from all the media;

Charles Morais of Desmeules Automobiles, Yves Simard of Sinutab, J.-Guy Guimond of Enterprises Guimond et Associés, Claude Joyal of Gestion Delpro Ltée, Michel Saint-Pierre of G. Lebeau Ltée, Edouard Mercho of Chomedy Radio, M. Audet of Abris Tempo, Serge Loriaux and Nicole Demers of Garantie Universelle;

Radio Mutuel, Simon Bédard of CJRP, Réal D'Amour, Richard Tremblay, Jacqueline Vézina, and Salon de la Femme, M. Terzini of the restaurant Le Café de la Paix in Quebec City, the Château Frontenac, Marcel Aubut of Le Colisée de Québec, Ronald Corey and François X. Seigneur of Le Forum de Montréal;

And all those who helped me morally and financially.

Diane Hébert
Diane Hébert Foundation
1080 Bélanger E.
Montreal, Quebec
H2S 1H2

Foreword

Diane Hébert's remarkable will and determination to live against all odds have left an indelible mark on all of us privileged to be part of her remarkable story. Her long journey from Quebec to California and back to Toronto finally resulted in a life-saving transplant. Faced with repeated post-operative complications, she underwent six major operations in a two-week period and, remarkably, emerged victorious. Since that time Diane Hébert has devoted herself to increasing public awareness of the need for organ donation, and the miraculous restoration of health which these much-needed organs make possible. Her story will leave a lasting impression on readers, just as her struggle to live has made a lasting impression on those who helped to care for her.

Joel D. Cooper, M.D.
Divisional Head, Thoracic Surgery
Toronto General Hospital

CHAPTER ONE

The Verdict

April 8, 1983

I am sitting here, breathless, in the cardiologist's office, looking out the window at a rectangle of impeccably blue sky.

"Is it as bad as that, Doctor?"

The time he takes to answer tells me immediately what the verdict is. He hesitates, looks at me, hesitates some more, then says gently, "Yes, Diane. I already told you, last time. You're going to have to give up all activity."

"What exactly is wrong with me?"

"Primary pulmonary hypertension...."

That doesn't help much. Especially the first word. Later on I learn that, in medical jargon, it means a disease whose cause is unknown. For the time being it's Greek to me. What I want to know now is:

"Could I die of it?"

"Yes."

This answer, one that should chill me to the bone, in fact stimulates me. I like things clearcut. I ask without any show of emotion, "How much time do I have? How long have I got to live?"

He looks at me again, hesitates again, and this time I'm the one to come up with an answer.

"Five years?"

He doesn't say a word, but shakes his head slowly.

"Four?"

The same helpless gesture. I decide to put an end to the countdown.

"Two years—that's it, isn't it?"

He doesn't contradict me. "It's not very easy to determine precisely...."

Nor to tell such a young patient she has so little time left to live.

I sit in silence for a moment, thinking. Two years' reprieve! That sounds like a reasonable remission. I burst out with incredible brashness, "Okay. I'll sell the house and furniture and take a trip around the world!"

Almost apologetically, he explains that the state of my health won't permit me to travel. He's right. For three years now, since the birth of my little girl, things haven't been going too well. I have frequent dizzy spells and I'm so short of breath I can't work normally. The first cardiologist I saw was reassuring. Nerves, he said, stress; a little rest and I'd be as good as new. But last January the manager of the store where I work, who had often seen me under the weather, got worried and urged me to consult another specialist. As soon as the second one saw the results of my tests, he advised me to give up my job, take oxygen, and get more rest. But I always insist on having my own way and I flatly refused to accept such a passive regime. My health would really have to deteriorate before I was ready to admit I was that sick.

In the cardiologist's little office we go on talking a while longer. The rectangle of sky is still impeccably blue. But I'm somewhere else. It seems to me that another person has taken my place with the doctor, is listening and questioning him without paying any attention to me. Finally, when the appointment is over, I leave like a sleepwalker and make my way to the car. It's a beautiful day. The sidewalks are dry. Winter is melting away. Birds are singing in the trees. I open the door and drop heavily into the driver's seat. It's spring, I'm twenty-five years old, and I'm going to die. The blue of the sky suddenly darkens and I can't see past the mist of tears. They claim a dying person sees the highlights of her life pass before her eyes in a few seconds. On the dark screen of my closed eyelids I see brightly coloured scenes of my childhood: summer in the country, the feel of grass underfoot, the chirping of birds, the treehouses I built with my five-year-old boyfriend, the cat I found and adopted and whose kittens I brought into the world—distant images of ordinary happiness. I'm still crying, but not for long.

Outside on Boulevard St-Martin cars and people are going by, completely indifferent. How many are aware of a cut-off point? How many know how long they have to live? Because they're all condemned, everyone dies someday. They're just lucky not to know when. I know. Two years! I haven't a minute left to lose, with life running away little by little. And already my instinct tells me to flee this sterile solitude and reach out to others. First, back to my job and my friends there.

But it's not easy to tell people you love that there's not much time left for you to love them. Behind their expressions of pity and compassion I can feel their fear of their own mortality. Seeing the tears they shed for me and with me, I'm almost tempted to console them, to reassure them.

Sharing my grief is a way to dilute and diminish it. It makes me feel better. Still, so much emotion tires me. Madame Byrne, my boss, who is a sensitive and practical woman, sees this and lets me take refuge in the accountant's office so I can order the oxygen tanks that will accompany me wherever I go from now on. Then—kindly, tenderly—she asks me to go home and rest.

Rest? How can I do that when the hardest and most painful thing of all remains to be done: breaking the news to Yves? He's only been part of my life for four months, but already he takes up all the room. In January, around the time the cardiologist first diagnosed my disease, we started living together. We'd only known each other about a week. Love at first sight? It must have been. And now likely to be no more than a flash in the pan, a love with no tomorrow, no future. We'll have to put a speedy end to our adventure. In all fairness I can't impose a life of uncertainty on him—what's the point of plunging deeper into a passion whose end is fixed beforehand? No. He has to leave me and lead his own life.

The thought of it blinds my sight again. Why me? Why should this happen when I'm just beginning to start over and get things going again? My marriage is finished, over and done with, its best memory my little girl, Isabelle. Undoubtedly the state of my health was the first cause of that separation. But the thought of going back to work and becoming independent again has given me wings, and for some time now I've felt as energetic as a twenty-year-old. I've started over, best foot forward, convinced that living with someone is still the best thing to do, even after a first failure. Yves has accepted everything: my divorce, the visits of my daughter, whom he already loves as if she were his own.... I think he'd be willing to stay with a dying partner—but I won't let him! As I drive on towards our little house in Fabreville, I try to find the right words to convince him that we should part without tears.

At home everything is neat as a pin. The breakfast dishes that littered the counter this morning have been washed and put away. There are piles of clean laundry on the table and the yard has been tidied up. My parents have been in again while I was out. For some time now they've been in the habit of taking care of my house. For how long exactly—three months? Four? Suddenly I understand the reason for their kindness. They know. The dates match: the results of the first tests and their first discreet helping hand. Now everything's clear. Their generosity...their care and attentiveness.... They knew. They know.

In fact, they've always protected me. I was their baby, their last little darling. Maman had six miscarriages before me. My sister is twelve and a half years older. I was pampered and fussed over, my least whims were satisfied—I was a spoiled brat. Whatever I set my mind to, I got, by either force of will or patience. My parents teased me gently: "You're stubborn as a mule," they'd say, laughing. It's true.

They were very afraid of losing me when I was six. I had to have surgery to the aorta and at that time they overprotected me. But the operation was so successful I was able to go back to school just like any normal kid my age. I was very active, liked sports. There were no after-effects, nothing that would lead anyone to suspect future problems. I can imagine their anxiety at seeing me threatened again. Powerless to challenge destiny, all they could think of was these little "house calls" to show me their tenderness. But the thing I want most now is something they're incapable of giving me. I want to live. I don't want to die!

Yves is here. I didn't hear him come in, didn't feel his approach. He looks at me, puzzled. My eyes are still full of tears. I'm not ready. The words and phrases I've planned so carefully are all jumbled, it's impossible to put them in order, to speak calmly. They tumble out anyhow. Yves seems shaken; he sits beside me on the sofa and we cry together for quite a while. At last I manage to explain to him that we have only one choice: to separate. He protests, asks for time to think things over; then, disbelieving, insists there must be a way, some hope somewhere.

"Is it really incurable?"

Then, little by little, the cardiologist's words come back to me.

"Just a minute, things are so mixed up.... At first I didn't pay much attention to him. He said something about California, about a heart-lung transplant being the only treatment. They've done quite a few operations in some place, I forget the name. Some were successful. But there's a long waiting list—fifty thousand requests a year. And the surgery and hospital care are very expensive."

Yves listens closely. I stop crying. So does he. He seems to be less sad. Just now he asked me for a day to think things over, but from the quiet way he says, "We're going to try everything, Diane," I know his mind is already made up.

CHAPTER TWO

The Warning

April 26, 1983

Today's my birthday. I'm twenty-six. It's supposed to be my lucky year, and I've been telling anyone who'll listen that I don't intend to start it in the hospital. I've been here a week already wasting the little bit of life I have left.

It all began with a sleepless night. I couldn't breathe and my body was in turmoil. It was as though I were trying to give birth to a hundred devils—my stomach was racked by wild contractions. I thought that it must be a bad dream, that I was going to wake up.... But I didn't sleep a wink. Beside me Yves dozed fitfully. It was still dark. Sitting on the edge of the bed, unable to stretch out, I tried to find a less painful position. No such luck. The pillows and cushions piled around me were useless. I'd exhausted my imagination trying out a whole series of ridiculous positions and contortions without the slightest relief. And I was suffocating. Quick! More air! I got up, hoping to breathe better. Even my oxygen tank couldn't supply my lungs. My legs were like putty, and when I stood up the room began to spin. By leaning on the walls I managed to make it to the toilet, where I threw up again, wondering what could possibly be left in my stomach. I had this mad idea that if I could vomit my lungs and heart up, it would be good riddance. I was totally exasperated, at the end of my tether, at the end of that tenuous thread that still tied me to life.

I don't remember how it finally got to be morning or how I ended up sitting in the kitchen. Seeing me bent over double, Yves was alarmed.

"Do you want me to take you to the doctor?"

"No.... You go to work. If it doesn't get better soon, I'll call Papa. I'll go to the hospital with him."

"Are you sure?"

I kissed him and tried to smile.

"Don't worry, it'll only be a couple more years like this...."

He didn't seem to appreciate my humour. Which was all right, because I really didn't feel like joking. I was scared stiff. I was thinking: this is it, I'm going to die, it's all over. As soon as Yves left, I called my father and waited for him on the floor, rolled up in a ball. The pain just wouldn't let go, no matter what position I was in. I think at that moment I *wanted* to die, just to kill the pain. When Papa finally arrived I sat there crying, huddled up in a corner. He'd never seen me in such a state. I'm not a softie or a whiner; I've always been very tough on my body. But this time I had no strength left, couldn't even stand up. He helped me to his car and drove me to Sacré-Coeur Hospital.

From there on my memories become confused. They must have given me tranquilizers. It seemed hours before anyone looked at me. Then doctors tapped, prodded, questioned me. I saw them discussing me, heard some of the words they were using: "Ovarian cyst, uterine foetus, acute appendicitis." Nobody seemed sure of the diagnosis.

"Are you going to operate?" I asked.

"Probably. That way we can see exactly what it is you...."

My nerves completely shot, I almost shouted, "I don't want you to! Somebody tell Yves, I want to see him first.... You mustn't put me to sleep...."

I was beside myself. Papa reassured me—he would let Yves know right away. Afterwards I must have fallen asleep, though I fought to stay awake because I was afraid I'd never come to again. When I opened my eyes I was in another room and Yves was there. He was saying he was sorry it had taken him so long; he'd had an awful time getting to the hospital—two traffic jams, trouble parking, and more trouble finding the right entrance. And then he'd been given the wrong directions: he got the wrong floor, the wrong corridor, and the wrong room—they'd kept him going from one wrong place to another.

But in one way the delay was almost providential. While he was looking for me the doctors had had plenty of time to study my dossier, and they had changed their minds. Because of my pulmonary hypertension an operation under general anaesthetic could have been fatal. They had also rejected two of the tentative diagnoses. What I had was an ovarian cyst, but I'd have to wait for it to disappear. During that time I'd have to stay under observation in the hospital. I protested vigorously.

"In the hospital? For how many days?"

"Perhaps two weeks...the time it takes to follow the development of the disease."

"But I can't. I won't! It's my birthday next Wednesday and I *won't* celebrate it in hospital!"

The doctors smiled at me indulgently. They took me for a spoilt, capricious child. Papa and Yves exchanged sly looks while I went on stubbornly repeating under my breath, "I refuse to have my twenty-sixth birthday in hospital."

I really believe that clinging to my whims and fancies like that made me survive. By desperately clutching at a date, at a precise time in my life that seemed auspicious and desirable, I had the impression I was pushing away death. I was eager to see tomorrow; I cherished, protected, and nourished this love of life that has never abandoned me, except in a few very rare instances. By looking forward to my birthday I set myself a goal and gave myself a new reprieve. Unconsciously, I was creating positive vibrations around myself; I was doing everything in my power to reach this new life-preserver thrown out to me, like a swimmer struggling to save himself.

A little later on, those convictions, still at a very intuitive stage, were confirmed when, at a meeting of the Club des Femmes d'Aujourd'hui, I met Céline Bastien. I was impressed by her calm self-assurance, and by the serenity that emanated from every one of her gestures. She's a teacher of relaxation, and we had several far-ranging talks together. She's a person who knows the art of listening and how to say just what's essential in very few words. We had never been close, so I didn't know when I telephoned her if she'd accept my invitation to visit me. She came to the hospital the very same afternoon and twice more that week. She taught me how to relax and how to create silence inside myself. I really needed that; my nerves were on edge and I was easy prey for any kind of pain. She made me see this and taught me how to conserve my energy and not dissipate it in useless tensions and fits of rage. She massaged me and spoke to me gently. We talked about death and my two-year sentence. She said, "You have powers within you that you don't suspect. If you really want to badly enough, you can give your body orders. Your body is an envelope, an instrument at the service of your will. It's your will and your will alone that can cure you." She brought me some tapes and suggested books to read. When she left I felt rested and the pain died down little by little.

That evening in my hospital bed, when everyone had gone, I did relaxing exercises before going to sleep. I repeated the words I forced myself to believe: "I'm going to get better, I can get better, I'm going to live." And then other words, more naive: "I'm going to celebrate my birthday at home." Every morning I spent a lot of time doing my hair and putting on make-up. Whatever happened I didn't want to look sick. My mirror must reflect a healthy, pleasing face, for others but also for me to see. Every day I walked a little farther in the corridors chatting with patients and staff.

Today I'm twenty-six. Just minutes ago the nurses brought me a birthday cake and gave it to me, giggling. I set the little cardboard box down beside my suitcase and put on some more rouge. In a few minutes Yves will be here and we're going to pick up Isabelle at her father's; then we'll all go home, where my parents will join us. I know there are birds on the trees outside. Today I'm twenty-six and nothing will stop me from being twenty-seven this time next year. If I will it, I can make it happen....

CHAPTER THREE

First Hope

May 31, 1983

My week's stay in the hospital had nothing to do with my pulmonary hypertension, it was just plain bad luck. My cardiologist assured me of this and explained in detail why I had so much trouble breathing—the arteries that carry the blood from the right side of my heart to the left are blocked, so they can't pick up oxygen from the lungs as well as they should. Phew! I've had to stick my nose back into my schoolbooks to brush up on the way the human body works. It's always amazing to realize how that little world inside us continues to function without our being aware of it. Something in all that escapes me and fascinates me at the same time, like the way my home computer works.

But there was something else that escaped me, too. How could I be sure of my cardiologist's diagnosis when another expert had seen my poor state of health as just nervous exhaustion? And for two whole years! Obviously one of them was wrong, but which? I certainly wasn't going to give in to the second verdict without contesting it.... So without either of the first two doctors knowing, I went to see a third, a specialist in heart disease. That way I'd see which conclusion suited me. The most reassuring prognosis always seems the best.

"We'll have to do a catheter examination," he said after examining me.

"Don't bother, it's already been done. I've got the results with me. Here they are."

He studied them a long time before going through my file. Then he got a little huffy.

"Then why did you come to see me? The conclusions are clear enough, and your cardiologist is an expert in this sort of thing. I know him personally. Besides, he took the trouble to consult his colleagues before giving his opinion. Look at those signatures. You should know we don't hand out a serious diagnosis without due consideration. I'm sorry—I can't do anything more for you."

He repeated what I already knew: it's generally difficult to determine the causes of this ailment, though in my case it might be due to a pulmonary embolism I had when Isabelle was born. That might explain why I never got completely well again afterwards. Anyway, I didn't care much about the causes; the disease was there and there was no medicine to cure it. The only way I could pull through was a heart-lung transplant and this kind of operation wasn't done in Canada yet. Consequently I would have to consider exile to the States for however long it took to find a donor.

But while having to go so far away from home was a little upsetting, the idea of resorting to an organ transplant didn't worry me. It seemed as simple as changing the motor in your car. I could never have put up with a slow, insidious disease, and I found the thought of dying in good health almost reassuring.

A little shamefaced, I returned to the Polyclinique St-Martin. My cardiologist there got the ball rolling by sending off letters to Stanford in California, where there had been a good number of successful double transplants. "It's one chance in fifty thousand," he told me. But what if I was the lucky one?

"You'll need lots of money."

"I'll sell my house and furniture."

12

"Lots and lots of money, Diane."

"What about Medicare?"

"I've written to the government. They'll probably reimburse the cost of the operation and hospitalization. But while you're down there waiting for a donor you'll have to pay for your own accommodation. Life in California is very expensive."

"I might be able to borrow a little...."

"You can also make an appeal to different service clubs and start up your own fund-raising campaign."

This suggestion didn't fall on deaf ears, nor did I waste any time. Yves helped me make a list of groups that might help and I began telephoning. Rémi Francoeur, director of the newspaper *L'Hebdo de Laval*, listened to me attentively. He's an active member of the Laval Optimist Club, a group that helps people in need.

"If Stanford accepts you," he said, "we promise to help."

"But why not begin collecting money right now?"

"There's no sense being hasty. Wait till they're ready to take you in California."

I was offended. I thought they wanted to get rid of me, or at the very least were refusing to take me seriously. There was nothing left to do but grin and bear it. And wait! My spontaneous reaction was to wish the time would go faster. But since my days are numbered, there's no benefit in seeing them speed by.

Still, I detest sitting around doing nothing. To give up all activity would be certain death for me—I won't do it. Despite the doctor's warnings, I continue giving music lessons...with my breathing tube and my oxygen tanks, that precious bottled air I can't do without any more. I use up to two litres a minute. Yves has installed an oxygen compressor in the middle of the house and this "air machine" with its 25-foot tube lets me move from one room to another all through the downstairs. My students say I'm brave. But what would you do if they told you you were going to die? Lie down and wait? Let yourself slip away quietly without a sign of protest? Not me! I'm alive and nothing will prevent me from thinking and acting that way. If that's what it is to be brave, then I guess I'm brave.

I refuse to sit home alone cultivating the blues. I go out in my electric wheelchair and drive around the block. The kids I meet are envious of this unusual means of locomotion. "You're lucky!" they say. I laugh with them. What's the use of telling them that I'd rather walk, that I'd much rather look after my house all by myself? A housekeeper comes in to help me with the domestic chores. Frankly, I don't like this situation. It's not easy for a naturally independent woman to have to rely on others. I'm no angel, I have to swallow my pride, but I grumble. I don't like the way the housework is done, but the cooking is varied and delicious. I try to see the good side of things.

I continue to be active in the CFAL (Club des Femmes d'Aujourd'hui de Laval). I take painting lessons, go to meetings, use the library. That's where I got one of the books Céline told me about when I was in hospital, *The Power of Your Subconscious Mind*. The title put me off—was it one of those books you have to decode with a dictionary? I leafed through it for a few minutes and was sure it wasn't the kind of book I like. I prefer novels and mysteries. Besides, there was a lot of talk about faith. I'm a believer and practising Catholic, but I don't go for ready-made prayers. I prefer to make them up as I need them. So I took out the book without much enthusiasm and left it lying on my bedside table for quite a while. Then one night when I was bored to tears, during the hockey play-offs, I picked it up the way you pick up a new medicine, looking it over skeptically before trying it, underestimating its possible helpfulness. The first lines left me cold, but as I turned the pages my prejudice dwindled. In simple language, almost childish because of all the repetition, Dr. Murphy talked about the merits of auto–suggestion. He explained how the subconscious mind, the force that controls the functioning of the organism even in sleep, is influenced by yes and no; how every organ reacts favourably to positive suggestion and, on the other hand, is harmed by negative thinking. In other words, if I repeat to myself continually that my heart and lungs are sick, my subconscious will set up a process of deterioration that will follow the orders it has received. Whereas if I do the opposite and assert that my lungs are healthy and my heart is normal, that good old subconscious will provide ways to improve their condition. Mere child's play!

I know I'm oversimplifying the author's ideas, but I just take what I need from his book, because I can't overlook anything that might help me survive. After a hasty reading of the first chapters I got into the habit of never going to sleep without first crooning a few comforting words to my insides. Here's the magic formula: to my heart I say, "Get back a healthy shape and colour." To my lungs, "Get clean and pink again." I don't put inordinate faith in these humble methods, but where's the risk? I have nothing to lose trying to win back my life. Besides, as I read through Dr. Murphy's book I discovered that the "Faith" he talks about is first and foremost an infinite confidence in the power of the will. If the Creator—call him Krishna, Buddha, God, Jehovah, or Vishnu—created man in his image, man must still have unfathomed resources within him, and the will is one of these unknown powers.

Everyone at some time or other has a chance to test that popular little saying, "You can if you want to." As far as I am concerned, I've often got what I wanted by sheer stubbornness. Afterwards I've just as often judged such mulishness to be very childish because of the effects it had on people around me. But here is an honest American, a doctor into the bargain, encouraging me to behave like a spoilt child. I'm happy to learn that my shortcomings have a good side and can be used like a double-edged sword.

Yves doesn't think much of my new-found philosophy. It's true that it's not all that different from the old one, and that it excuses all my whims. For example, when I say, "Yes, I want to do this or that tonight," he invariably replies, "Slow down. You're wearing yourself out. You go tearing around as if you had the devil by the tail. Why can't you relax a little?"

"But I want to. If you don't want to come, I'll go alone."

"Boy, are you pigheaded!"

He looks at me impatiently, but I know he'll give in because he wants to go too. Yet I don't really lead him around by the nose. He sometimes has the last word, and if he decides not to give in, I have to postpone my begging for a while. But only for a while— I'm totally incapable of giving up some of my desires. Luckily our disagreements don't set us off against each other too often, even though we don't share the same tastes. For example, he'll settle down in front of the TV while I go to my meetings with "the girls", and I don't have to endure his rock concerts when I have my earphones tuned to another station. We cohabit with our differences intact and, naturally, share many pleasures together. In fact, I think he likes me precisely because of my stubborn determination that opens every door ahead of me.

This morning at breakfast I felt very strong pains in my chest. Tears came to my eyes. In a rage I said, "I've had enough.... I want to live!"

Yves didn't budge, didn't say a thing, just looked at me. And in his eyes I saw not pity, not sympathy, but a kind of confidence—I wouldn't go so far as to call it admiration—as if he were saying, "Whatever it is, when you want something you always get it...." Then he left for work as usual.

Now here I am pacing through every room in the house. The pain has subsided at last. I've watered the plants, fiddled with the keys of the organ. I don't feel like playing this morning. Don't feel like going out either. I've got nothing lined up today, and I feel as glum as if I were waiting for something that would never come. And yet it's almost summery outside. The neighbour's cutting his lawn; there are dandelions on ours. On the highway opposite the cars are tearing along both ways as if they were rushing to get to some celebration or other. I sit here dully, watching them dash off God knows where while I'm tied to my oxygen tank as if to a ball and chain. How could I feel anything but imprisoned? In my nose the air is fresh, almost cold. Come on, heart, pump; get pinker, lungs!

In the street the kids are racing their tricycles. The postman has stopped next door. Will he stop here? Will I finally get some news? Try as I may to avoid thinking of it, my heart starts pounding. I desperately want to hear my dog yapping the way she does every time she hears footsteps on the front steps. Go on, Gigi, bark! Run after the postman, bite him in the leg if he hasn't got a letter for me. That's it! She's growling, I hear the noise, now she's really barking. The postman walks across in front of the window, and when he sees me and hears Gigi, he pretends to run as if he were being chased by some nasty mutt. He smiles and gives a friendly wave. I burst out laughing; this little scene has tickled me.

On my way to the letterbox I make plans for the rest of the day. Think short-term; live from day to day. Every minute counts; I must savour each one as if it were the last.

In the mail, under a handout from some pizzeria, is a big envelope from Quebec Medicare. I hold it a minute without opening it, devoured by gnawing doubts. What if it's a no? Is there any way I could change their decision? I read my name on the envelope. Someone I don't know has written to me; someone who doesn't know me either. Someone has studied my dossier, has classified me, decided for me. What will the verdict be? Do I deserve to live, according to them? I feverishly tear open the envelope and as soon as I've seen the first few lines I know what it says. They agree to pay the cost of the operation and hospitalization, but at Quebec rates. If I'm admitted to Stanford, they add.

Hmm. They seem skeptical too. It's as if everyone doubts my chances.... Not me! I rush off to share my joy by telephoning my parents, Yves, my friends. Because in my own mind there's not the shadow of a doubt: I will be admitted.

CHAPTER FOUR

Living in the Present

September 26, 1983

The summer has sped by without paying any attention to me. No letter from California in the mail. Every time I visit my cardiologist I ask him, and every time he answers patiently, "I'll phone you as soon as I have any news." I've put my hope on hold and, forgetting that every day brings me closer to the cruel deadline, have chosen to live my last two years happily. I don't bother with the countdown. Every morning I repeat, "There's two years left," as if trying to hang onto time, as if I could win this race against the clock. I even get to thinking that by lying this way I'll somehow cheat destiny and scramble its plans for me. It's sheer presumption on my part, but isn't that the privilege of the condemned? To believe that at the last moment the noose will come untied and the hangmen will remove their masks and slap their thighs and roar with laughter, "Hah! What a great joke!" Who hasn't dreamed that? What prisoner hasn't seen himself flying out his cell window? What paralytic hasn't woken up sure he's going to get out of bed and walk out the door? Just wake up and dismiss the nightmare? But this breathing tube keeps me from forgetting I'm sick. Sick? Even I have to remind myself that if I can't run or walk the way I want, I can still talk, sing, laugh.

When my thoughts turn black and things are at their worst, or when I'm overcome by anger, I lock myself up in that little room completely filled by the organ. As soon as I put my fingers on the keyboard and press down, the sound thrills me and carries me away. My voice rises clear and sure above the sonorous notes. It seems to me that my whole body winds itself around a long ribbon of sound. I don't think any more, I don't suffer, I am pure voice. My obsessions, my fears, my rages, my desires all filter mysteriously into my mouth and drift up in a long kind of prayer.

I remember my panic when the parish priest first asked me to replace the organist. I was twelve and full of blushing adolescent shyness. I had never played in church and didn't know any religious songs. "That doesn't matter," he said. "You can just play *L'eau vive* and other popular songs. Come on!" I can remember shivering when I played the first notes, and the echo that reverberated like my own hesitation. But little by little I got so used to this solemn sound that I became a regular organist for Sunday mass. For weddings too; funerals were too lugubrious. That's how I got my first paying job. It's a lucky thing to discover at age twelve that work can be pleasant and remunerative at the same time. Besides having a small salary I had a group of people who listened to me, I can say it literally, religiously. I like to share my love of music. My neighbour often tells me with a laugh, "Leave your window open, I adore hearing you sing." I'm glad to. I can spend hours on end escaping this way.

I don't care if Yves doesn't appreciate my repertoire and prefers rock and songs with a heavy beat. He thinks I'm out of date, old hat. It's true, I grew up with the refrains of the forties in my ears—romantic songs, chansonnettes, and dance orchestras. It's my romantic side. It's what saves me from being a perfect tomboy and brings me close to people of an older generation. I communicate with them easily thanks to this complicity. We

19

both experience the same nostalgia when we hear those old-fashioned tunes. I like young people too, of course; in fact I like to be surrounded by people all the time. I'm the sociable type while Yves is rather solitary. That's the most important difference between us—I don't see any others likely to create problems. Up till now Yves has supported all my decisions and the cardiologist's proposals. He doesn't act impatient, though I sometimes sense he's anxious and tense. I'm often afraid to see him following me into this adventure. What if he loses two years of his life?

But I drive away these gloomy thoughts. Yves is big enough to know what he's doing. For that matter, he's a head taller than I am. It hardly surprised me at all the first time I met him; he was the same height as my husband. Was it a sign from fate? We chatted together for a couple of hours one night in that mixed dance hall–piano bar–discothèque where I'd gone to escape boredom. I'd only been working a little while, and I found my new liberty stimulating and scary at the same time. I was stepping outside my solitude very cautiously and had no desire to start living with anybody. Yet Yves pleased me immediately; he was everything I wasn't—calm, considered, imperturbable. From my miniaturized point of view he seemed to be a gentle giant. When I refused to give him my telephone number, I was relieved to see him scribbling his own on a scrap of paper. "I'll be seeing you!" he said, and his tone of voice didn't leave any doubt that we'd meet again.

A week later I hovered at the telephone with the piece of paper in my hand. I hadn't spoken to Yves about my divorce or my daughter. I'd have to put him to the test. I dialed the number (he was living with his parents) and had to wait a long time before he came to the phone. As soon as I heard his voice I blurted out an invitation for "a drive with my daughter". He didn't seem surprised to be chaperoned. He said he wasn't doing anything and would be right over. In my book, he'd passed the test with flying colours.

My parents arrived unexpectedly just as I was leaving to get Isabelle at her father's, and I asked them to look after my guest while I was out. So it was my mother who opened the door when Yves showed up. Still shaken by my recent separation, she wasn't too keen on meeting a new suitor. The first contact, then, was cold—not to say icy. But that way, without planning it, I'd killed two birds with one stone. Daughter, family, everyone was there, and Yves knew them all from the start. I had avoided those formal presentations usually reserved for one's parents. Not that mine are unpresentable or anything, but since they had a tendency to be very suspicious of anyone who showed an interest in me, I'd never have dared hope for such a quick first meeting.

Was that what hurried events along so? After that day in the sun and fresh air, with Yves and Isabelle playing happily in the snow together, I for one was ready to start up a new threesome any time. I invited Yves straight out to come and live at my place. He didn't say yes, didn't say no, but on each of his visits he brought over a few more of his belongings, very discreetly, as if he were afraid of inconveniencing me by moving straight in. In reality, he didn't want to shock his parents by leaving home too abruptly. I appreciated this sensitivity. One day towards the end of January he informed me that there was nothing left to bring over. He'd decided to stay for good.

It's eight months now since he entered my life, on tiptoe, carefully as a cat. For him, too, the two-year sentence is a threat, and like me he keeps pushing it away. Is my life richer because I know it will be short? Sometimes I have the sensation of being alive so intensely that I believe, absurdly, there are certain advantages to knowing my fate in advance. The pleasure of existing, of feeling the freshness of rain on my forehead, the taste of fruit on my tongue, the powerful smell of earth rising on the autumn air, all those things I took for granted now take on extra value because I'm in danger of losing them. "Let's live every day, every hour, every minute, as though it were the last," Yves says. And I add, "Let's make our craziest dreams come true."

So we make plans together. The idea of a trip around the world has left me little by little. I have very modest ambitions for someone who's going to die. I dream of a house on a big piece of land covered with apple and cherry trees. With spacious rooms, a playroom for Isabelle, a fireplace downstairs, and cats purring on every cushion. Green house-plants climbing up wide windows and flowerbeds in front of the house. Nothing lavish or unreasonable, just a welcoming sunny home. Yves and I spent the first months of summer visiting houses, and since I didn't like any of them well enough, I drew up some plans and took them to an architect. We're going to buy some land in the country not too far from Isabelle and build our dream house there. It's decided— Yves agrees. He has even anticipated me, and to please me has built a rock garden right here behind the house, big black and grey stones with a profusion of flowers in pastel shades.

Apart from these short-term projects, I forbid myself to look ahead. If I don't think about tomorrow I manage to be perfectly happy. Well, almost! I miss Isabelle. Yves and I only have her one weekend in two, and it's not enough. I feel my daughter growing away from me, feel we're out of touch. Then I get mad at my infirmity, at not being able to take care of her. Every time I see her she seems to have grown. She seems to be gaining in strength all that I'm losing in energy and fitness. It's as though, to have one of us live, the other must inevitably pay the price. It may be natural for an old woman to see her daughter take over her place little by little while she gently dwindles...but Isabelle is still a baby. She needs me—I feel it, I know it.

It's the kind of thought I absolutely mustn't linger over. In four days she'll be here. I'm tempted to spoil her, to anticipate her least wishes as my parents did all through my own childhood. Would I be so determined and confident if they hadn't acted that way with me? If I've got this will to live inside me, it's their doing. Will my daughter be like me? Will she be as capricious and difficult? I'm almost tempted to hope so....

For her birthday I bought her some presents that I'm going to wrap up in a minute. I like anniversaries: they're rituals that link us to the past and yet are full of promise. I let my thoughts wander. What will Isabelle be like at four? At five? Then I stop modestly. I can't look ahead so far; it's forbidden.

Friday will be the most wonderful day in the world. I'm going to make it an unforgettable birthday. I've bought lots of brightly coloured balloons and paper favours. I'm going to wrap the presents beautifully and use lots of ribbon.

I've got the things spread out on the kitchen table: a box of Lego, a doll, modelling clay, candies. But what's this? A sheet of paper I didn't notice when I came in has just slipped under the table. It's a message from the cleaning woman: "Doctor F. asks you to call his office." Underneath is my cardiologist's number. It's ten to five, I've just got time. Strange how fast my heart is beating all of a sudden. Didn't my doctor tell me during the last routine examination, "I'll phone as soon as I have any news"?

CHAPTER FIVE

Passport to Stanford

October 1–10, 1983

How could I do anything but attract attention with this breathing tube hanging off the end of my nose? In the 300-seat Lockheed 1011, people are looking at me quizzically; I can read the surprise on their faces. I can imagine them whispering, "She doesn't look sick.... What do you think is the matter with her? And him, he's so attentive, you can tell they're in love...." A little more in that vein and you'd think I was on my honeymoon. Some honeymoon! But Yves and I have never taken a plane together before, and despite the unusual circumstances it's hard to hide our excitement.

I look over at him and ask, "Haven't forgotten anything?"

"No. And you?"

"No." I prod my chest. "I've got my old heart and the same old lungs, that's the main thing. That's what the doctors want to look at."

I laugh. He finds my realistic attitude hard to take. He takes my hand.

"Listen, Diane, I think I did forget something after all."

"What?"

"To say I love you."

I kiss his moustache. It's so good to be two. To glide effort-lessly through the sky alone in this mechanical bird.... Well, not exactly alone, since dozens of eyes are still spying on us. I try to hide my happiness and remember my cardiologist's words: "Don't forget, Diane, these are only preliminary tests. You're not admitted yet. It could be a long wait...." Nevertheless I have the impression that this ten-day trip to California is the start of an adventure. A very strong feeling tells me to interpret it that way. I feel confident, the way I did when I was writing my final exams. But these reflections are cut short by a young man in uniform asking us some questions.

"Wait here, I'll be back," he says.

"Okay. We weren't going anywhere."

Don't worry, cabin steward, I'm not going to step out the door. I could run short of oxygen out there! But what's he up to? He comes back and asks us to follow him.

"The plane's not full," he explains. "There are some seats in business class. You'll be more comfortable there."

We are. The seats are wider, it's not so stuffy, the neighbours are more discreet. During the whole flight, offered to us courtesy of Air Canada, we are treated like royalty, not exactly what either of us is used to. So here in the clouds somewhere between Montreal and San Francisco, the little girl from Ville St-Michel dines with silver cutlery off fine porcelain, on tender roast beef and spring vegetables. And from a crystal goblet I drink a little toast, just an excuse to say a joyous "*Santé!*"

I wonder if I owe this special treatment to my breathing tube or to my smile. I know people don't usually associate sickness with good humour...yet the pleasure of eating well, of laughing and talking, seems to make me forget the worst; I have the feeling I have a gift for happiness. Is it because we're flying so high? All during the flight I feel carefree and very, very light.

But I'm made up of the same fears as everyone else, and when the plane slows and starts coming down on a landing field that seems to be all *water*, I hold my breath with the rest. Even Yves, imperturbable Yves, looks scared. Out every window all you can see is ocean getting closer and closer...we're headed straight for it. I close my eyes and panic. I know I couldn't swim; I'd never escape from an accident like this. I find myself stupidly thinking that it would be too bad to die this way since I'm already condemned. I make up a little prayer: "Hey, up there! Not so fast. I've still got two years left." It must have registered. I recognize the slight shudder of a plane touching down before it bumps along the runway. Land! Here we are at our destination all in one piece. Phew! Afterwards they explain that the airport is on San Francisco Bay and the runway is close to the water. They could have saved their breath—I'd figured that out already.

This nerve-racking landing brings us up short against reality. Someone's waiting for us at the airport. Quebec friends, Nicole and Bernard Baumier, have told a mysterious stranger we're arriving. Nicole spent some time at Stanford and got a new heart there. She recommended this man's company during our stay in California. "You'll feel very out of it at first. Chuck Walker is exactly the man you need," and she gave us a photo of a smiling young man with a beard. It's just like a detective story. I avidly scan the faces around us, all the more eager to meet him since I know he had a transplant of the same type I'm going to have. I'm curious to see how healthy he looks. Finally I recognize him; same smile, same sparkling eyes. He comes over—he must have seen my breathing tube—and shakes hands warmly. The first thing that strikes me about him is the hand I'm shaking: no thumb, and five fingers almost all the same length. It doesn't seem to bother him. He's already talking to us as if we're old friends, takes me by the arm, looks after our bags. I've never seen a man more energetic. Now I see why Nicole insisted on our meeting him. Chuck was the second heart-lung transplant in California, and in the past two years he has resumed all his activities: he has two jobs going full steam, drives his own car, likes to act the ham, takes a glass with the best of them, and is quite the lady's man. He's Stanford's most remarkable success and also the most talkative—a real chatterbox.

Yves casts a crestfallen glance my way. Like me, he can only understand about two words out of three. We suddenly realize we're in an English-speaking city with no linguistic resources beyond what little we gleaned in grade school. I translate as well as I can: "Motel, nice, good place, not expensive," and while he drives us over to this oasis Chuck goes on talking *trop vite*! Too bad, because his jokes fall flat when you only catch half of them. Seeing his impish eyes smiling at me in the rear-view mirror, I know I'm missing a lot. I swear I'll learn English like a shot.

Yves is sitting there silently, looking at the scenery with big childlike eyes. He's never seen California, and all this luxuriant vegetation, the heavy traffic, and the invisible presence of the sea—almost palpable in the light and air—are like a dream come true. My own childhood memories are quite confused— palm trees and swimming in the ocean, that's about all I can remember of a trip with my parents. I too take in the Stanford University campus wide-eyed as we drive quickly through. Then our friendly, unintelligible guide leaves us at the door of a motel whose comfort is much more modest than its price.

All during our stay Chuck was our tireless driver, now acting as guide, now as interpreter (with incredible difficulty!), and always with wonderful good humour. "He's so funny!" says Yves. "Imagine what it would be like if we understood him!" I promise him that one day we won't miss a single one of his jokes. I was too optimistic—as luck would have it, we were never able to communicate fully with Chuck. But I don't want to anticipate, so I'll return to the day after our arrival, when the three of us went to the hospital for the first time.

Chuck leaves us at the reception desk with a booming "Good luck!" Just when we're beginning to get used to his accent, here are half a dozen others, from the south, the mid-west, the east, leaving us as mute as a pair of goldfish. I finally manage to understand that these preliminary examinations don't require any hospitalization, so we'll be free to do some sightseeing between tests. Blood samples, X-rays, lung tests, electrocardiograms, echographs—none of these things frightens me; I know the ritual, I went through it all in Montreal. But I must admit that having to translate into English what I feel when I'm blowing into a tube and someone is prodding me in the ribs makes it even harder not to laugh. Especially when the doctor questioning me is extremely British and has kept the accent and the special sense of humour. He makes these long, boring examinations seem some kind of a game, which adds a carefree air to our visit. Except perhaps when an echograph examination that normally lasts half an hour stretches out to an interminable three and a half hours, because the doctors can't get over the way my heart is beating. They've never heard such a hammering. I feel like telling them that I'm used to it, and reminding them that that's why I've come, for a change of heart and lungs. But not right away, since this battery of tests is just a necessary control before getting admitted to Stanford. When I learn that I won't know immediately whether I'm accepted or not, I protest and insist on an answer. I find the words I want: I tell them Yves and I deliberately lengthened our stay so we would know before going back. "We'll do the best we can," they reply, when faced by my determination.

But I'm confident. The hospital is as small as its reputation is great. Its resolutely modern air and the efficiency of the staff reinforce my positive thinking. Besides, I know my dossier is a good one. Apart from my heart and lungs, all my organs are in good shape, which is an indispensable condition for transplant surgery. I am also assured of strong moral support during the different stages of the procedure. Just before I left Montreal a psychologist met all the members of my family: my father and mother, Isabelle, and of course Yves, who didn't escape these investigations either since he's ready to follow me all the way through my adventure. What I don't know yet is, will I be sufficiently different from the other people waiting for a heart-lung transplant? Because the Stanford team choose their patients carefully according to their exact needs. That means that my blood type, my tissue morphology, and the size of my rib cage will all play a decisive role in their choice. They will have to be different from those of the fifteen other patients who are also afflicted with some incurable disease. That way they hope to get a varied sampling so the patient's constitution will coincide as exactly as possible with that of the potential donor. I'm counting on my small size and my lucky star.

While waiting for news after four days of tests, Yves and I spend our time by the pool of a second "nice, good place, not expensive" motel. The weather is wonderful and, to the great surprise of the Californians, we have no hesitation about swimming during this first week of October. The local residents have long since folded up their deckchairs and parasols as if the sidewalks were ankle-deep in fallen leaves. For us it's still summer. Yves swims like a fish; I'm only allowed the occasional little dip because my heart and lungs won't take total immersion. But so what? I can tell the climate's good for me. The tall eucalyptus trees waving their perfumed leaves overhead seem to help me breathe. With Chuck we explore the surrounding countryside. We visit Palo Alto, the little town Stanford is in, and drive down to the Pacific at Santa Cruz. On the jetty a few fishermen are out teasing the fish, while sea otters snort in the waves not far from them. Seagulls wheel in the blue sky. What peace...what music!

"Oh Yves, wouldn't you say time's standing still?"

"No. It's four o'clock. Just time to go and get changed before supper with Jimmy and Huguette."

"That's right. I forgot."

Jimmy and Huguette Dewarvin come from the north of France. A year ago Jimmy came to Stanford hoping to get a new heart. But the treatment he followed and the medicines he took progressively improved his health to the point that he's now cured, he assures us. He and Huguette have taken a liking to the California lifestyle and have bought a big house at Menlo Park, a wealthy suburb of Palo Alto, and they're living out their American dream with their daughter. They're great people and they've quite simply gone native, wearing the relaxed t-shirts and wide-checked pants of their new neighbours. It's almost a surprise to hear them speak French. But the thing that delights Yves and me even more than their language is their cooking. To eat French is a gastronomic adventure, from the *entrée* to the *mousse au chocolat*—not forgetting the cheeses. After such a memorable meal, how could we ever refuse their kind invitation to come and stay with them while we're looking for an apartment? "If you're admitted," Jimmy adds.

"I'll be admitted!"

"You seem pretty sure of yourself."

"Well, not really sure, but I think I've got a chance and I'm hanging on to it. I really believe it."

"Anyway, if Diane isn't accepted here," Yves says, "we'll go and try some place else. There are other cities where they do this operation."

"Maybe, but the success rate is very high at Stanford."

"That's why I'm here, and I know they'll take me."

"I don't doubt it for a minute," says Huguette. "You seem so determined to live, just like Jimmy was before he was admitted."

"I'm certain everything's going to work out."

"Me too," says Yves when we leave our new friends a little later. "It seems we always meet the right people at the right time."

True enough. What could be more encouraging than Jimmy's case—curing himself with just a little medical assistance! It reminds me not to give up on my technique of auto-suggestion. But just so I don't go putting all my eggs in one basket, I'm not forgetting the example of Chuck Walker either, still alive—and so full of life, too!—two years after a heart-lung transplant. So turning the light off that night I make a double wish: to get better *and* to come back to California soon to wait for a donor.

Two more days go by without news. It's only on the ninth day, just before we're due to go back to Montreal, that the phone rings in our little room in the El Rancho Motel.

"Mrs. Hébert?"

"Uh...yes...that's me."

"It's okay. You can come back in ten days."

"Ten days...? What do you mean, ten days? Not so fast! We have to sell the house, get our things organized...and the financial backing.... Do you think they can get things going in ten days? You must be joking!"

"What's that you say?"

I take the time to translate and the doctor, out of sympathy or simply tired of my confused explanations, agrees to lengthen the time.

"By how much?" asks Yves.

"I've got to be back in two weeks. It's crazy, Yves. We'll never make it!"

"Don't worry," he says rubbing his hands together. "I'll get you here!"

CHAPTER SIX

Heroine or Victim?

October 20, 1983

Like every little girl, I suppose, I've often dreamt of being
famous, of having my picture in the papers, of being recognized,
respected, and loved by people I don't know but for whom I
represent some sort of ideal. And like most little girls I did
my dreaming without really believing in it. How could I have
guessed that one day I'd make the front page of the morning
papers because I had an incurable disease?

Here they are all around me, photographers, reporters, boom-
men, sound men, cameramen, and journalists. In my stomach
there's that kind of knot they call butterflies, that indefinable
state between fear and excitement: fear of not being able to find
words, of being understood poorly or not at all, but also the
excitement of being listened to and watched. As I go on speaking,
however, my voice regains its edge, and I my self-assurance. I
don't have to make up a story, mine's already there—I just have
to put it into my own words, simply, taking care to be accurate.
I've been warned that media handling is like shunting freight-
cars—sometimes facts get lost in the shuffle—so to avoid any

risk of confusion I make a point of answering every question and never hesitate to repeat myself or to amplify any detail I'm asked about. I'm not afraid any more; out behind these microphones and cameras are people listening with their hearts. My message comes across loud and clear: to live I need the financial support of the whole population of Quebec. Besides the cost of the operation and hospitalization, which will be partly covered by Quebec Medicare, it's estimated that my stay in California will cost between forty and fifty thousand Canadian dollars.

This press conference is the kick-off for the fund-raising campaign. All during the summer, while I was concentrating on living in the present, a team of people was quietly working behind the scenes preparing my future. As soon as I sent out my call for help last May, Pierre Francoeur got in touch with Dr. Michel Dallaire, president of the Laval Optimist Club. Immediately seeing what was needed, he got together a solid, dynamic team of people with varied backgrounds. Each helped according to his competence: Maître Jean-François Martel looked into the legal side; my cardiologist took care of the medical aspects, and Pierre Francoeur contacted the media. Even before I knew if I'd be admitted to Stanford, they had carefully planned their campaign. This strongly optimistic attitude certainly contributed to the fulfilment of my ambitious hopes: without being aware of it I was already surrounded by positive vibrations. When I finally told them the good news, everyone was ready and the machine swung quickly into motion. One obstacle remained: because of long bureaucratic procedures it wasn't possible to set up a duly constituted foundation in such a short time. But the Foundation of the Sacré-Coeur Hospital was willing to lend us their secretary and treasurer so it was possible to send income-tax receipts to anyone who made a contribution. Then, within a few days, hundreds of service organizations operating in Quebec were informed of the campaign, and many of them, including the Laval Police Association, decided to help.

Today representatives of the media—the press, radio and television stations—have been invited. They've come in little groups and have set up their tripods and apparatus. Sitting in my lap, Isabelle is shy and scared. She can't understand why so many people are suddenly interested in her Mama's old heart. I explain to her that it's no good any more and that I have to go far away to get a new one. She says that's okay as long as I come back to her really soon. That's my wish too, that it be just a few months, whatever the cardiologist says. He multiplies the three months I count on spending in California by six.... Well, we'll see!

Yves stays slightly off to one side. The organizers of the campaign have recommended discretion; the image of the mother and child alone will go down better with the media. He doesn't object to staying on the sidelines; in fact, I think he prefers the position of privileged observer. He listens and watches like a cat, keeping his thoughts to himself. But I know how deeply this adventure affects him. For that matter, he looks tired. He certainly hasn't been loafing around since he quit his job as a refrigeration technician. As soon as we got back from Stanford he was busy with a dozen things. He doesn't mind telling "our story"; he told the manager of his credit union, and soon every branch will be displaying my photograph. Besides that, he's emptied our house in Fabreville in no time flat. We were lucky enough to find a buyer quickly, a neighbour who'd had his eye on it for years. In less than a week Yves sorted out everything into two rooms, the contents of one to take with us, the other to stay here. Of course we'll only take the minimum: a few clothes, sheets and blankets (is it always warm there?), dishes, kitchen utensils, appliances, a few books, my computer (I have to have some fun, don't I?), and the TV, which will surely help us learn English. Will all that fit in the car? It'll have to. Yves is leaving in two days, on October 22, and will take all this stuff to Palo Alto. When he gets there I'll already have arrived because I'm leaving by plane in four days.

Everything else, including the furniture and the organ, has been taken over to my parents' place. They've been nice enough to turn over their basement and other rooms and corners to us. My dog, Gigi, will stay with them or with my godparents; my cat will go to Yves's parents and my plants will continue their lives with friends. People around me do everything they can to help; I bathe in an atmosphere of comforting solidarity.

My parents didn't hesitate to interrupt their lives by taking Yves and me in while we wait for our respective departures. Despite all the confusion of the move they also consented to have the press conference here. They're here too, a little put off by the thirty-odd intruders who keep bombarding me with questions. Papa, discreet as ever and sparing of words, keeps sending me sympathetic and encouraging winks from behind his glasses while Mama answers the journalists' questions. I know how uneasy she feels receiving so many people in a home already overcrowded by a double quota of furniture. Like the careful, tidy housekeeper she is, she's concerned for her reputation. I feel like telling her, "Don't worry, Mama, they only have eyes for Isabelle and me."

Because all the cameras are focused on us. We're the subject that later, through the photos, will touch so many hearts...the pictures of me bending over my daughter with my breathing tube, that double symbol of life and death, between us. But I would gladly do without the artificial air for a few minutes just to project an image more like the one I have of myself! I've already admitted it, I'm vain, I detest looking sick, I refuse to solicit pity. So I concentrate on acting healthy, even though the journalists seem preoccupied with my imminent death. I reply to their questions as honestly as I can. "Am I afraid to die? Yes, just like anyone else, I guess...but this trip to California is a chance to survive, and I believe in it." Is it just my imagination? They seem skeptical, disbelieving. So, to reassure myself as much as to convince them, I add: "When I come back I'll dance for you."

It's that defiant little phrase that I like best when I look through the papers over the next few days. The photos so clearly chosen to play on people's emotions don't stir in me the feelings I dreamed of when I was a child; this heroine looks more like a victim, sad and resigned. Yet it's thanks to these images that the fund-raising campaign meets its goal. Thanks to them, but thanks also to that little phrase I blurted out—a cry of hope.

CHAPTER SEVEN

Life Ahead of Us

October 24–28, 1983

Time has been galloping. Now that Yves has gone I'm left to my own devices. I have to sort things out and pack, answer dozens of telephone calls, and see family and friends before I leave. And plan all those last-minute things that take hours to settle. I haven't got time to think; I'm whisked away in a whirlwind of activity.

In the halls of the airport I'm preceded and followed by journalists. I recognize some of them, can put names to their faces. There's already a web of complicity forming between us. Some of them will even be making part of the trip with me, so I may as well get used to them. Like so many of the people who turn around to watch me go by, who recognize me and remember my story from the papers and television, they are caring and attentive. Little did I know four days ago, when I asked for financial aid from the people of Quebec, that they'd be so generous with their moral support too. I can tell from their expressions and their words of encouragement that they're following me in their thoughts on this hazardous journey.

But my parents don't take kindly to this intrusion on our privacy. Mama's tears are heartfelt and Papa's anguish is painful; neither of them likes to display feelings in public. Especially when the cameras linger over their distress. Even if the trip is full of hope for me, they can't help worrying about the consequences. And California's so far away. I can guess what they're thinking, without daring to say it: "Parting is dying a little."

On the contrary, I am undertaking this journey to be reborn, and despite the pangs I feel at leaving them and Isabelle, I don't feel any real sadness. The consideration shown me on every side chases away any morbid thoughts. I'm learning to live with the interest people show in me, though I don't appreciate yet what a help it will be. In satisfying the curiosity of others I free myself from my own fears; in reassuring them I reassure myself. For me, talking is a kind of therapy.

I indulge myself to the full on the way from Montreal to San Francisco, because I have a travelling companion who sets me up perfectly. She is Suzanne Martel, president of the Health and Community Services of the Laval Red Cross. Officially she insists on keeping her title of nurse, but in fact during the following week she is more properly my guardian angel, interpreter, press agent, and confidante. I'm glad to be travelling with her. We gossip together like a couple of old cronies and manage to forget completely what we're doing here. The illusion is perfect: she's no more my nurse than I am her patient. We're two friends flying to California on a holiday. As on the first trip, the aircrew are most attentive; again I'm the guest of honour at their little party. In such conditions how could I feel the least bit worried or nervous? There's just no time for that kind of nonsense. Everything's so pleasant that the flight speeds by and we're landing before I know it.

For the next four days I find myself back among friends. As promised, Huguette and Jimmy have offered Suzanne and me their wonderful French hospitality, with swimming pool and Californian palm trees thrown in. Our sun bathing is interrupted, however, by numerous activities. Suzanne and I continue the explorations I began with Yves. We do a lot of window-shopping but I manage to be quite prudent. I need plenty of clothes and other things, but how long will I need them for?

One visit to the hospital is enough to bring me back to reality. Without ceremony they hand me a little gadget to wear on my belt at all times. It's my "beeper", to tell me if they've found a donor for me. As soon as I hear the signal I'm to call the hospital and be ready to go there immediately. On this visit I receive the official title of "recipient", which, with a touch of humour, is what they call people waiting for a transplant. So here I am on the list of patients with nothing to do but wait patiently. Suzanne translates the doctor's orders: there are no particular obligations, just a monthly visit to see that I'm in good health. So we now have plenty of time to look for an apartment near the university health centre.

Unfortunately, that's not so easy at this time of year. The students are back and have taken up most lodgings near campus. The yellow pages and want ads aren't much help. With Chuck as our good-natured chauffeur, we drive up and down the streets of Palo Alto, the little town surrounding the university. At last it's Suzanne on her own, after many disappointing visits to places too small or too dirty—oh yes! even in California—who turns up our first home.

"Listen, it's no dream, but it's modern, clean and sunny."

"Is the apartment big enough?"

"Well, for a couple of love-birds like you it should do."

"How many rooms?"

"It's a studio, Diane. One room with a kitchenette and a sleeping area. And a bathroom, of course."

"Is it expensive?"

"Yes, very, like everything we've seen since the start. But I'm afraid you don't have a choice."

"How much?"

"$775 American."

"*What!*"

"Yes, and it's not furnished except for the stove and fridge."

Suzanne seems as upset as I am. But when we go over to 1380 Oak Drive the next day, I don't hesitate for a second. The neighbourhood is inviting, with big apartment blocks buried in greenery. There's a huge willow in front of the building and a forest of oaks with a little stream running through it quite near by. From the tiny balcony there's a good view of the hospital and up Willow Road. What more could we ask for? Space? Sure, but how would we fill it with our meagre belongings? A bigger apartment would look like a desert. Besides, we'll only be staying here a few months....

So it's decided; I'll take it. The view is pleasant and the room is airy. A few pictures of Isabelle on the walls will freshen it up and give it life. I haven't got time to fritter away anyway. Not far away, a Radio-Canada team is waiting to interview me with Chuck. Réal and Pierre, camera and microphone in hand, have been following everything I do. Thanks to them and the TV screen, my parents have been able to keep track of my daily life. If I hurry up a little maybe the team will be able to film our new home before they have to go back to Montreal. Oh, come on, Yves, get here quickly. I need your strong moving-man's arms.

Back at Huguette and Jimmy's I make a list of indispensable purchases: a bed, a table, chairs and an armchair. That's the minimum. Huguette watches me, smiling. "I've got everything you need," she says. "I've even got a love-seat I'm not using." How good it is to have friends! They make everything seem so easy. Ever since I left Quebec, it's been one surprise after another. I feel as though I'm living a happy dream full of astonishment and gratitude.

When Yves finally turns up on the 28th of October, I proudly show him my acquisitions. I must confess that sometimes I'm cruelly thoughtless. Here I am waiting for him to congratulate me on finding a place to stay and things to furnish it with, oblivious of the fact that the trip, which for me only lasted the length of a conversation, for him stretched out in interminable lengths of monotonous roads and complete solitude. He does look washed out. He's aged by five days and five thousand kilometres. His eyes have that worn look cowboys' eyes have, and he moves with the distant calm of truck drivers. His speech is slow and riddled with silences....

His trip began badly. Already exhausted by the two moves, he was in pretty bad shape before he started. On the Macdonald–Cartier Freeway on the outskirts of Toronto, his nerves gave out. His body, sorely tried during the previous few days, couldn't take it any more; his mind couldn't either. As though it were the car that had broken down, he pulled up on the shoulder. He had to empty himself of pent-up feelings of despair. He'd been building up all sorts of unacknowledged fears and repressed exasperations. Now he had to allow himself to put everything back into question—his love, his tenderness, the whole Californian adventure. Suddenly the thought of going off to play nurse under the palm trees became ridiculous; the whole trip seemed grotesque. Knowing that you can't reason yourself out of an emotional crisis because your logic starts to backfire, Yves just let himself go utterly. Until there were no tears left. Then he started the car up again and drove on. Having got this far, it would have been absurd to turn back. You never know what it is that pushes you to choose the unknown. Maybe it's the attraction of the end of the tunnel that draws you towards new landscapes, despite yourself.

So he continued on his way, only stopping to eat and sleep. But even here, he ran up against some subtle language problems. It seems easy enough to ask for a room for the night: "Have you a room to let? A bed to sleep?" They gave him a long hard look before letting him into the motel. Even at McDonald's they laughed at him good-naturedly when he asked for "a hamburger *avec fromage*". He'd end up laughing too and would finally find the right words. But when you're travelling twelve hours a day—without any passengers, because there's not even room to open the side window—you keep talking to yourself *en français*. And it was in French that he went through customs. Lucky for him the officer hailed from Lacolle, Quebec, and understood that he'd forgotten to register his precious cargo on the Canadian

41

side. Because without that he risked paying duty on his own sound system, TV, camera, and toaster—all "made in U.S.A." but bought in Canada—when he came back. But the officer was friendly, he used the same toothpaste as Yves, and America turned out to be that vast country where everybody understands a smile. "Don't worry your head about it—*bonne chance!*" he said.

As the journey progressed, magic signs appeared by the roadside: ones with sporting associations—Detroit, Chicago—others that spoke of other kinds of folklore—Dubuque, Des Moines, Cheyenne. Between the cities, the solitude of the fields stretching away to the horizon with a few farmhouses dotted here and there like mushrooms. And near every town the same fast-food strip, the same billboards.... What was there to be homesick about?

The spectacular scenery came later, after Salt Lake City, where the landscape changes abruptly and stretches out like a flat golden sea. It was only there that Yves's head began to clear of all the questions. From then on the final destination didn't seem so urgent, or rather it came nearer with every mile. The car seemed to be teleguided, drawn down to the presence of the invisible sea. The road cast its spell. His body worked by reflexes. It was the last leg of the trip....

I have been listening to Yves without interrupting. Though he is drunk with tiredness, he's been talking for a long time, incapable of shutting down the flood of words that has been building up inside him for almost a week. Now he's drowsy. I suppose that even in his sleep he keeps on driving on towards some point on the horizon. The mystery between us deepens. I can see that our differences are much greater than the two kinds of trip we've just experienced: Yves interiorizes all his emotions while I live all mine out on the outside, as though I'm afraid to let them penetrate me. It's my way of surviving. My instinct tells me not to dwell on things. Like a butterfly I flit from flower to flower, from one idea to the next. I don't explore things; I remain on the surface. When I ponder over things, I get depressed. That's forbidden.

Yves does the thinking for me. A good thing, too, if he's decided to go on doing it. When he was away, I didn't think about him. I lived like a scatterbrain. If I haven't sought a single minute of solitude since he left, that's part of my instinct for survival too. I've tried to find in others the things I like so much in him—his calm, his assurance, the way he thinks before he speaks. In fact, I've been waiting for him impatiently, spreading myself thin just to make the time go faster. I didn't miss a single chance to forget the waiting that had already lasted far too long.

Now I'm happy. He's here and I can stop fidgeting and snuggle up to his shoulder and relax. I can tune my breathing to his and find our old rhythm, that stimulates him and calms me. Tomorrow we move into our little lovers' nest. Tomorrow I'll act as if we had the whole of life ahead of us.

CHAPTER EIGHT

Settling In

November 10, 1983

Before eleven in the morning it's impossible to know if the weather will be fine or not. Thick fog transforms our apartment into a pilot's cockpit: the cloudy green you can see through the window makes you feel you're floating in mid-air, and the rest of the scenery is absent, rubbed out, hidden in mist. The suspense lasts all morning. And then, imperceptibly, the miracle takes place: the sun appears, wide awake and already high in the sky, and, like a painter amusing himself, in its own good time it sets about colouring in the landscape. First the black trunks of the trees, then the green of the foliage, then the red and blue of the cars rolling up and down the boulevard like so many toys. This is the reason, naturally, we have decided to get up at eleven, just in time to see the fog disperse. Since we came the weather has been uninterruptedly marvellous. It's a heaven-sent gift these two Québécois can't get used to. We can scarcely believe our eyes. As soon as lunch is over we set up our chairs on the balcony.

As if to rival this Californian generosity, the folks back home have offered us a present too. A big box, wrapped and tied to withstand any blizzard, was waiting for us in the mail room. I was as excited as a kid, but I made the pleasure last till we were safely upstairs before opening the mysterious package. It was a regular treasure chest—not one present, but hundreds— Yves swears he counted more than three hundred—from every corner of Quebec. No, no, not chocolates or peppermint candies. Each present is individually signed. With that as a clue, it should be easy to guess.... They're letters! On white paper and blue, lined, squared, or plain, hundreds of unknown people have taken the trouble to write. They send messages of encouragement and admiration expressed in tender, sweet, pious words—real love letters. They're the most wonderful present I've ever received.

Sitting on the balcony Yves and I carefully unfold the pages. In every tone imaginable it's the same wish: "Don't give up, come back home completely well again!" In fact, I have been feeling better for some days now. Is it the marvellous climate here or that strong wind of friendship blowing from Quebec? I don't know. At any rate I can go for several hours at a stretch without my oxygen tank. It's also true that I've been going on with my positive thinking to strengthen my heart and lungs.

Besides, Yves has taken over full-time care of the house. In no time he had arranged the furniture Huguette and Jimmy lent us and unpacked our bags. That cut down our living space somewhat; it'll be touch and go whether we have enough room to live together without too much friction. In any event, it's easier in daytime than in the evenings. If we don't go out for a walk in the afternoon, the balcony acts as a second room, small but airy, a place where we can be alone, each in turn. But that's not possible in the evening, and I find myself exposed to interminable sports programs—Yves alone knows what a lot of them there are on American TV. I put up with them, but I grumble.

To his credit I must say that my football fan has developed an extraordinary zeal for everything concerning *la cuisine*. Like all sons of good cooks, he was incapable of getting a meal together at first, but he's made surprising progress in the pasta and tomato sauce line, and now chicken holds no secrets for him. Besides, I secretly suspect him of preparing for a career in the pastry field. At the same time every afternoon he puts on his best hotel waiter expression and asks, "What would you like for supper tonight, darling?"

"Chicken, sweetheart."

"Chicken again? I made that Monday."

"That's all right, you cook it so divinely I wouldn't mind having it every day."

"Okay. And what about dessert?"

"I can't think. Do you know how to make a cake?"

"Yes...I guess so."

"It's easy. Just get a mix and add milk and an egg."

"A mix? Never! My first cake will be strictly homemade."

"Whatever you say, but...."

Yves has forgotten that the only sugar we have is in those little paper packets that are so practical for coffee or tea. When the recipe calls for a cup and a quarter of the stuff, it takes the patience of a clockmaker to unwrap enough one-teaspoon doses. He has also forgotten that our only sieve is about as big as a thimble. For a first try, however, I must admit it's a success—although the dessert comes long after the meal!

"Mmm! Delicious! Will you make me more?"

"I promise."

He seems to be sincere. I notice he's added several things to the shopping list and I wouldn't be surprised to see sugar and a sieve among them.

This way time sifts slowly away like sand in an hourglass. When there's no sports on TV, we try to improve our grasp of the language of our new neighbours. We can follow and understand the detective shows on television—not a very sophisticated level, granted, but they teach us terms not often used in our everyday life. Our first English lessons are our dialogues between good guys and bad guys, gangsters and police. It can't be all that effective because we still argue in French.

"Turn the volume down, Yves. I can't hear myself think!"

"What do you mean? I can barely hear it."

"It's too loud!"

"That's what *you* say."

Not even a door to slam to stop the argument. It's sometimes hard for two people to live together without a wall to separate them.

"I'm going to buy some partitions, some screens, some...."

"You'd be better off buying some earplugs if you're so sensitive!"

"*Earplugs!* You're the one who should be getting earphones.... Yeah, go ahead and get some earphones, Yves. I'll even pay for them!"

Since it's a question of my health I think I can afford the purchase. And besides, we're not on quite such a tight budget now. Along with all the other letters in the surprise box was a message from the Laval Optimist Club. No, not a message, rather a business letter stating that the fund-raising campaign was in full swing and that results had far outstripped our expectations. If things go on this way we'll soon have enough to meet our needs for two years.

"Wait a minute, I don't want to spend the rest of my life in California! Three months will be plenty, won't it? It seems as though we've been waiting around here for centuries already...."

"Come on, Diane. We've only been here two weeks."

"So? That young guy who got here the same time we did has already had his transplant."

"He was lucky, that's all. Listen, you don't expect people to die just to offer you their heart and lungs, do you?"

"Of course not! But lots of people die with healthy organs that could save other lives, mine for instance."

"You're reasoning like an egoist."

"No, I'm a realist."

This last affirmation falls on empty air. At least we have the wisdom not to insist too much, not to start repeating ourselves. Because in this kind of argument words quickly begin to bob up again and again. He's right though, I am selfish, and impatient.... But my nerves are shot. My beeper went off twice this week, both times breaking rudely into my dreams in the middle of the night. It's a terrifying sound, as raw as a police siren.

"What's that, Yves?"

"Huh?"

"Is it the police or a firetruck?"

"It's your beeper, Diane."

My beeper. That's right, it's going "beep-beep", and I'm scared stiff. Quick, call the hospital and tell them I'm ready for the scalpel, ready to turn in my old heart and lungs...*beep*...*beep*.... I can see the surgical gloves, the doctors approaching with living organs to neatly replace mine. Quick, I want to live. Quick, dial the number!

"*Allo? C'est l'hôpital?*"

"...?"

"*Allo?*"

"Yes...?"

Oh, that eternal language problem, always having to think in English. It's amazing just the same how well I can express myself when my life is at stake. Amazing too how quickly I understand that this particular dream has just gone up in smoke.

"Diane, why are you hanging up?"

"It's a false alarm, Yves."

"What do you mean?"

"Oh, I don't know. I didn't pay attention to their explanations. A thunderstorm set the signal off or something like that...."

Both times it was the same scenario, the same emotions, the same disappointment at the end. Just thinking back on it makes my heart gallop. To calm it down I go back to my letters. Some of the messages are very short: "Be brave. I'm thinking of you," signed Jean-Pierre. Or "*Chère Madame*: I don't know you but I read about you in the newspaper. I think you're really courageous. I'll pray for you." And at the bottom of the page in studied handwriting: "An old grandmother who thinks of you every day." No name, no address. Others, on the contrary, give lots of details, share the letter-writer's troubles, bring up events from the past.... "I know it's not much compared to what you're going through, but just being able to tell you does me so much good...."

It helps me too. I breathe better because of these letters; they're like a big breath of love reaching me.

"Do you realize that, Yves? People I don't even know think of me every day."

"You're lucky."

"What about you?"

"Well, what about me?"

"Aren't you lucky to have me right here beside you all the time?" I say, laughing. He doesn't reply. He's sometimes quite miserly with tender words, but that makes them all the more appreciated when he does say them. After all, isn't his continual presence by my side a tangible proof of his tenderness for me? Doesn't he look after me, care for me like a baby, do the housework and the dishes? He even takes care of our birds. He's installed a feeder for the humming-birds, those magnificent little flying jewels. Sometimes our balcony looks like an aviary with all the jays and humming-birds. I've always adored animals, since I was a child. When I was small I looked after a regular menagerie of dogs, cats, squirrels, mice, chipmunks, turtles, and birds. But it's the birds I like best of all. They're so free. So dependent too.

"Look, Yves, there's that bluejay that was eating out of my hand yesterday. He's crazy about peanuts. I recognize him because of that black spot on his beak. Look! He's going to eat us out of house and home."

"That's not him, Diane. This one's got plain wings and the other had stripes."

"You think so?"

"I know so."

I'm certain I'm right, I have an infallible memory for this kind of detail. But so what, we're not going to start arguing again. And since the bird comes over and eats out of my hand, isn't that proof enough? Now he's flown over to a branch of the big willow. The fog has completely lifted and the wind is ruffling the leaves. It's going to be another superb day.

"It's a sin to sit here doing nothing with such a sun out there."

"Are you a mind-reader, or what? I was just going to suggest going out somewhere. I want to move around a little."

Yves's face lights up. I know what he's thinking.

"How about a little trip to Santa Cruz?"

"If you like...."

He pretends not to care but I know he's dying to go. He loves our excursions along the coast as much as I do. At least we share this fascination with the sea.

"Just give me five minutes, time to put my face on, and we'll go."

"Okay. I'll get out the wheelchair."

It doesn't take much to make me happy. I feel really good today. I smile at myself in the little round mirror on the table. A pleasant face looks back, skin lightly tanned, eyes sparkling mischievously. I'll have to be serious for a moment while I put on my lipstick.... Ah, how clumsy I am. I've dropped it and it's made a smear. A noise made me jump—a noise I refuse to hear, a noise that goes on despite me. *Beep...beep...beep....*

No, I won't. Not now. I'm not ready. This isn't the right moment.... If only...if only it's a false alarm!

CHAPTER NINE

The Meeting

November 25, 1983

In one week my beeper went off five times, mostly in the middle of the night. You'd think it was doing it on purpose. Just when I'd finally managed to drop off—I sometimes have trouble getting to sleep—it would decide to let go with its damned beeps. Even when the batteries had run down it would still churn out its inhuman message: *Beep...beep...beep...*. You never get used to the fright; every time there's the same anxiety. What are they trying to do, give me a heart attack? At the hospital they gave me another beeper. Since then, no more false alarms, and I'm calmer. I'm well aware that the signal ought to overjoy me. It would mean the end of my waiting, wouldn't it? But it's given me too many false hopes. Too much expectation has evaporated too quickly, too often. So now, irrationally, I don't want to hear it any more. I want to forget it, want it to shut up, want it to let me sleep, to let me dream I'm alive.

Of course, I'm not the only one to be woken up this way. There are as many stories about beepers as there are patients waiting for transplants. During the first meeting of "heart-lung recipients" I hear some pretty hair-raising ones. There are twelve of us around the table; Yves is with me. At last I'm going to meet some of the men and women going through the same anguish. They are all, like me, living on borrowed time. The medical team has chosen us for the variety of our physical characteristics, but in one crucial way we're all the same: our days are numbered. Yet at that casual meeting their faces don't carry the least sign of worry. They don't look sick or hopeless. They look like people you'd meet in any crowd, neither more nor less preoccupied. Some of them act in a very off-hand manner, cracking jokes and laughing easily. You'd almost think it was some kind of family reunion.

Unfortunately, I don't participate as much as I'd like to—that damned language problem again. Hunt around in my dictionary as I may, these Anglophones still speak too fast. I'm always a joke behind. When I catch on, they're already laughing at the next. Here and there I catch a word I know, but I have to resign myself to missing the full sense of what goes on. Too bad, I'll learn.

We go around the table and introduce ourselves. When it's my turn I make a point of stressing my origins. This comes as an astonishing revelation. For them, obviously, everyone in North America speaks the language of Ronald Reagan, at least as a second language. They're so totally convinced of this they even go as far as intimating that I manage pretty well in English. But I'm sure that compliment is just to reassure me, for they all automatically start talking more slowly. One after another they introduce themselves. Howard Brandon, Loreen White, Andrea Matsushima, Lonnie Austin, Judy Holden, Jerry Austen, Debbie Rosenburry, Penelope Tony, Debbie Mora. They come from the four corners of the U.S.—from Texas, New York, Oregon, Nevada. In this sense they're strangers too, as they insist on telling me. Even if they're not foreigners, they're all a long way from home. A few of them are with their families; others, like me, have a bodyguard—a spouse, friend, or close relative. Most of the latter have found temporary jobs nearby. Yves hasn't been so lucky: he hasn't got a work permit. His voluntary services will be reimbursed, so to speak, by the generosity of the people of Quebec, who continue to support us financially and morally.

Despite these slight differences, Yves and I are welcomed by the group. There will be meetings like this every month and we will feel more and more at ease in them. So in the long run we will form a sort of family. I'm looking for a more accurate word because there is no authority figure at these meetings. I mean nobody assumes a paternalistic or maternal role. There's no envy or jealousy either. I see for myself that the Stanford medical team has indeed chosen its patients carefully. None of us is in competition; no one is waiting for the same type of donor. No one is suffering from chronic defeatism either. On the contrary, these are people endowed with a tremendous appetite for life; these "recipients" are made of stainless steel; they're go-getters, superactive types, never-say-die people. Not heroes, no...or if they are, their heroism is within reach of everyone.

It's thanks to these meetings that I discover I'm one of them. Once again I'm led to believe in the usefulness of my stubborn-ness, knowing how indispensable it is to my survival. With my new friends I laugh at my whims and at their excesses. Some-times, these meetings get to be more like good parties than anything else, with a few bottles of wine doing the rounds too. Yves, the loner, will make some friends here; he needs to.

This first meeting has the good effect of taking us out of our solitude. Beyond Chuck, Jimmy, and Huguette, we don't know anybody in California. Of course our parents telephone and write regularly, but that's not enough to fill the big empty space that takes up the middle of our lives. I've always had a busy social life, and I find these long periods of semi-solitude hard to take. As for Yves, he's beginning to feel the bad effects of idleness; the routine of housework, cooking, and TV is getting boring.

It's refreshing to see all the new faces around the big confer-ence table. Most of the women, who don't like looking sick any more than I do, have taken the trouble to put on a bit of make-up. After the rather formal presentations, the atmosphere becomes more congenial. Despite our difficulties in translating our impressions, we more or less manage to understand each other. Americans are curious and they ask a lot of questions, which we answer as well as we can. I think our awkwardness invites a more sympathetic hearing. We chat for a long time with Debbie Mora, a sociable talkative young woman. She's from Texas and her second husband is living in Los Angeles with her children. For the Thanksgiving weekend he'll be coming over to see her. Would we like to take the opportunity to meet him? It's an invitation we can't refuse.

So a few days later Yves and I find ourselves in the middle of a real family. Debbie's husband and father are there as well as her sister and her five children. We are joyfully welcomed by this gang to their mobile home—a very popular type of dwelling in the U.S. Despite the cramped quarters, the table is set for a feast. Here Thanksgiving is almost a religious holiday. Before the meal we all hold hands and bow our heads while Debbie's father says grace. Yves and I are moved: the simple, warm atmosphere and the steaming turkey surrounded by delicious side-dishes remind us of Christmas dinners, and the presence of the children, as noisy and curious as a flock of birds, strengthens the illusion that we're back in our family again. In fact, for several hours we have the impression we're visiting distant relatives. It's only as we leave the long, narrow house and recognize the Californian vegetation and scenery that the dream dissolves.

This first evening in the company of someone in my own situation is a memorable one for me. Is it because Debbie was the first to offer us her friendship? A rapport was born between us that night. Alas, it didn't have a chance to develop—for less than three months after our first meeting Debbie was dead, before having her "chance".... In the language of Stanford, that means the chance to have her transplant. During that long weekend when so many highway accidents always happen, we talked about our chances. I know this attitude may seem cruel and egotistical to someone in good physical condition, but for all those whose survival depends on the death of someone else, it's only realistic; not to wish for more fatal accidents, of course, but to hope they will save other lives.

If I take this opportunity to look ahead in my story, it's to illustrate the difficult reality we were living during our Californian stay. After this first meeting when Yves and I met our fellow adventurers, we were constantly confronted by the death of our new friends. We were like passengers on a bus. Some would get off during the journey, either to have their "chance" or simply to leave, having waited in vain. Others would replace them, sharing the same faith in their destiny, showing the same incredible determination. We shared, this way, the risks of the human adventure. By the February meeting three of the nine patients we had met in November had left their places to others. Three women, three unlucky ones! Fortunately, all the statistics were not so sombre, and there were remarkable success stories that kept our hopes up.

For example, on that evening of November 25, when Yves and I returned to our little studio in Palo Alto, we had news from Carl Ruppe, the young man who had arrived at Stanford the same time as I. He had had his operation on November 5 and was soon to leave the intensive care unit. According to the doctors, he told us, he would be able to go back home before the end of the year. So I was far from thinking that Debbie, whom we had just left, was celebrating her last Thanksgiving.

I am, we both are, in high spirits. The family turkey dinner has reminded us of our own holiday preparations. My parents and Isabelle are going to spend Christmas with us. At last I'll be able to see them and hold them close. I want it to be an unforgettable visit. Quick now, finish off the list of presents, get the house decorated, prepare the fold-out bed for the visitors. Suddenly there are a thousand things to do. It's as though we have just awakened from a long sleep. Time was dragging; now it starts to fly. At least that's the impression we have, talking far into the night. We dream aloud. We'll buy a real Christmas tree; Yves will make a cake; I'll hurry up and finish the little painting I started more than a week ago. Despite the lateness of the hour I can't get to sleep. I feel feverish. I try to calm down, to find a comfortable position, relax, breathe slowly. But I have to get out my breathing tube, which I've been using less and less. It's because all of a sudden I've become so impatient. I want this first California Christmas to be an imperishable memory. I *want* it so, and it will be. Because I can't help thinking it might be the last. For better...or for worse....

CHAPTER TEN

Merry Christmas!

December 15–31, 1983

Winter here is the rainy season. The canopy of the sky stays grey and the sidewalks are almost always wet. It becomes a little trying. Even in December there's not a single snowflake. From which you can guess how far the Christmas spirit has to go to get Californians to swallow all those frosted greeting cards. It's funny they haven't got around to decorating the palm trees or putting Santa Clauses in the swimming pools. No, I'm joking. In this season there's no difference between our stores and theirs; the same sparkling snowy decorations everywhere. It's only the shoppers in shorts who remind us that we're in a warm climate. It's true we've had all the time in the world to make comparisons. What hours we've spent looking for the cheap little detail that will transform our apartment! For example, we found some nice brightly coloured tablecloths to put over some cardboard boxes; our guests will think they're end-tables. It's not that we're on such a tight budget, but I'm being careful. Who knows how much longer we'll have to spend here? Anyway, I'm economical by nature, used to counting my pennies and not throwing money out the window. It's one of the great principles of my education: "Always spend less than you earn!"

Every month the Laval Optimist Club sends us a cheque for $1,500 issued by the Diane Hébert Foundation. This amount corresponds to what the expenses of a couple living in California are estimated to be, as calculated by a Stanford social worker, Mary Burg. More than half of that goes to pay the rent; the rest is for electricity, telephone, food, gas, and minor daily needs. I faithfully send in all the bills to show that the money hasn't been dishonestly wasted.

So we haven't got much to throw around, though there's no shortage of temptation when we walk down those aisles more crowded with good things than ever. I thought I'd be able to resist all the holiday tricks, but I finally caved in, though it wasn't clothing or perfume or jewellery that grabbed me. No, it was a piece of furniture that would have gone very well in our studio— a little bulky, it's true, and not especially decorative, and to tell the truth, not too easy on sensitive ears.

To justify my whim, after everything I've just said about how economical I am by nature, I must explain that for us Christmas has always been a celebration of song and music. From the age of twelve, as soon as I knew how to play the organ, I got into the habit of bringing the family together around the instrument; it's become a kind of tradition, a loving union between the music, my parents, and myself. Obviously I wasn't thinking of that when I saw one of those compact models standing in the mall of a shopping centre. I wasn't thinking of anything; I was simply fascinated. I rolled my chair right over to the organ, pushed the stool aside, and began to play. I don't know how long I'd been playing when I turned around to see that I was surrounded by a group of curious bystanders. Was it because of my wheelchair? Then a salesman came over and congratulated me. Next he praised the qualities of the little organ and took me inside to show me other models. "You can have one delivered tomorrow," he assured me. It was a great temptation because even in English I understood his explanations perfectly: the little one outside was second-hand; he'd let me have it for a song. Yves wasn't with me; he sometimes draws the line at shopping and this time a friend was with me, one of those I've made since that first meeting with the other transplant recipients. So I called my man to find out what he thought of such a bargain. At first he just seemed impatient with me. "It's crazy, Diane! You know our budget won't allow us to...." But when I assured him that Papa would certainly offer to pay for this as a marvellous Christmas present, he left off preaching. "Do what you like!" he said, giving in. So I had my way and bought the organ. And I often go back to the store where they let me play the bigger ones.

That's how I got to know Kenneth. He heard me playing several times and one day he struck up a conversation. He loves music too and that's what we talked about at first. Then little by little we discovered something else we're both passionately interested in: fishing. To begin with, hearing me dreaming out loud about the deep-sea excursions we'd make and the huge fish we'd catch, I think Yves was jealous. But Kenneth has too much white hair to be a serious rival, and for that matter he's over sixty and has a wife, who works in the shopping centre where we first met. He's retired and spends his free time travelling and practising his favourite sport. I immediately chose him as adoptive father, a role he could hardly turn down because he had just signed on as department store Santa Claus for the holidays.

It's always remarkable how easily one thing leads to another after a first encounter. Besides making a friend, without really looking for it I found the perfect person to make my daughter happy too, for Kenneth gladly accepted to join us for our *réveillon*—in his work clothes, naturally. Isabelle is even luckier than most kids because her Christmas is being filmed for television. The Radio-Canada team turned up at our place again on December 19. Isabelle and my parents had arrived four days earlier, and we'd just had time to get them settled and show them around a little. In fact we pushed our Christmas gift-giving ahead somewhat so it can be shown on Quebec TV on Christmas day.

I'm glad to be able to offer my Québécois friends this present; it's a way of thanking them for their interest and generosity.

Everything is happening just as Yves and I planned: the tree, the Christmas cake, the decorations, and above all the thrill of being together again at last. For a few minutes I forget the cameras completely and really have the feeling of being back home again. Maman cries a little, Papa wipes his glasses, and I'm moved too. Isabelle claps her hands and kisses Ken's fluffy white beard. Yves smiles at me. I'm on top of the world. Couldn't we just stop the clock right here? Push the pause button and let the trembling image linger? No. Time is unjust and pitiless. It seems to run at top speed through those moments we prepare most carefully.

Fourteen days after my parents' arrival it's that familiar, inevitable journey to the airport.

"We had a lovely time," Maman tells me in the car. "Yves is a wonderful guide. Too bad the weather wasn't better.... Thank Chuck for lending us his apartment. And don't forget to write to your aunt. When I get home I'll send you the newspaper clippings. You look tired to me.... No? Well, dress warmly, it's quite humid outside. It looks to me as if you're catching a cold."

I don't answer. I'm all upset at the idea of seeing them go. Isabelle hugs me close. She's in one of her moods, distant and inaccessible. All of a sudden she's taken refuge in another world I can't get into. You can only imagine what a child's suffering must be like when they haven't enough words to describe it. But I can guess what she's feeling. Me too, I've been spoilt with tenderness, I've had an overdose of happiness. I hurt all over. When I kiss Isabelle one last time, when I free myself from her little hands, it's as though my heart were leaving me. Tears come spontaneously. It's a release, a "morning after" reaction.

There's depression in the wind for both Yves and me. The excitement of the preparations to greet my parents, all the activities and excursions and the emotion of leave-taking, have tired me out. Yves too is exhausted. But you can read something else in his face. He's bored. He's homesick. December is the hardest month to spend far from one's family; that's what he tells me later. The rituals of Christmas soften the toughest of us, and Yves is far from being insensitive. In our little studio suddenly grown too empty we comfort each other. Is he discouraged? Then I boost his morale, and when he's up again I allow myself to sink down a little. Those are the rules of the game, the ups and downs of the couple's balance-beam.

Luckily we have friends, old and new: Kenneth and Dorothy, and Johanne and Pierre Drapeau, a couple from Quebec living in California. And the Christmas cards and letters of encouragement continue to pour in. You'd think the whole of Quebec was participating in my adventure. Journalists from the papers and the radio phone regularly to keep their public up to date. A current of solidarity builds up that touches me deeply and helps me keep my hopes up, and theirs. My parents tell us of other proofs of affection. I can't get over the interest I seem to arouse. Since her return to Montreal, Maman has practically spent days on end on the phone giving out news. Is she keeping her spirits up? Good! Tell her not to let us down. I hope one day I'll deserve their confidence and be able to prove they were right to believe in me. Even if I sometimes have my doubts....

Little by little we're learning to live in another country, helped by the discreet charms of our life together. Sometimes it only takes a tiny thing—a bird landing on our balcony railing, a ray of sunshine breaking through the heavy morning fog—to fill the day with promise. But there are other days as black as the one when, after feeding the jays and watering my plants, I learned of the sudden death of Loreen White.

"Do you realize, Yves, she's been waiting two years...."

"Is she the one we had Thanksgiving with?"

"No, no. That's Debbie. Loreen was much sicker. You could tell she didn't have long to live. Oh Yves! She waited two years...two years for nothing. Yves, I'm scared."

He looks at me. He knows exactly what I'm thinking.

"Listen, Diane, she was unlucky, that's all. Some people wait much longer and still find a donor."

"Two years! I wouldn't have the patience, the strength, the health...."

"Don't say that. You don't know. Nobody knows. Don't think about it. Think about Jerry Austen instead. He came in July, he was operated on in December, and he's fine now."

"Yes. But he's a man. Do you think men stand a better chance?"

"There are no statistics showing that, it's just an idea you've got. Don't think about it any more. Tonight the old year ends and a new one begins, full of unforeseen things. Why start thinking it will be a bad one even before it's begun? Listen, don't worry about the old year.... Turn the page!"

"I'd like to, but it's not easy. Put yourself in my place..."

Yves doesn't answer. I sit down quietly at the organ and begin to play. It's the only way I know not to think of anything. I don't even notice him going out. He comes back much later with his arms full of packages. I can see him taking a bottle of wine out of one of the bags. He bangs pots and pans around in the kitchen. He didn't even ask me what I'd like for dinner. So I'm taking it out on my computer—I've just won two games of Trashman.

Good smells start floating through the apartment. I've barely had time to work up an appetite and here's the chicken on the table, home-made french fries, gravy, salad.... All I have to do is pull my chair up.

I laugh: "How did you guess?"

"Guess what?"

"That I was looking forward to chicken!"

"It's easy. It's always the same."

"No it's not. Tomorrow I want filet mignon."

"If you want."

"You know, you're right, Yves. Tomorrow is a new year. It's like a snow-covered road, a road to take together. I want it to be as if we were reading a book, I want to turn the page at the same time as you."

Yves lifts his glass.

"Okay. But first let's finish this chapter with a toast: *Santé!*"

"*Santé!*"

CHAPTER ELEVEN

Just for Fun

January 20–21, 1984

Nobody knows precisely how long I'll have to spend here. Since the first of the seventeen heart-lung transplants performed at Stanford—that is, since March 1981—the waiting period has varied from five days to two years. It's impossible to draw any conclusions by taking an average of those seventeen cases, there are too many factors involved. It's all a question of compatibility between the recipient and the donor: blood group, tissue type, size of organs. So it's just coincidence when a young man like Carl Ruppe, who has a very rare blood type, waits less than a week for this very rare operation. The case of Chuck Walker, Stanford's number two, is every bit as exceptional. Chuck's rib cage, like mine, is very narrow, an uncommon thing for these big strong Americans. Yet he was in California for only two weeks before they operated. He received the organs of someone very slightly built. So average-sized recipients aren't necessarily luckiest, even if their chances are better.

All this information picked up from meeting others, from reading, and from the TV can't answer the question that continues to torment me: when will my beeper go off? When can I at last telephone Dr. Jamieson and tell him firmly "You have a donor? Good! I'm ready!" I've gone through every scenario possible, but since turning the question around every which way doesn't bring me any closer to an answer, I've finally given up that game.

So I'll just have to wait as long as need be. The fears that troubled me at the time of Loreen White's death have evaporated. My health has improved considerably since I arrived; being free of stress and living in this mild climate have certainly helped build up my strength. I'm even ready to bet I've still got two years left despite the eight months that have gone by since my first sentence. Who could contradict me?

But even this resolutely optimistic way of thinking has no effect on the passage of time. Time hangs there like a huge flat sky, uniformly grey, the colour of boredom. I'd like to blow the clouds away. But I can't. Even with Yves's lungs I couldn't. So I say:

"I need a change. I want to have some fun."

"How about doing some painting, or playing the organ? I could leave you alone if you like."

How considerate he is....

"No, I want to go out somewhere!"

"Okay, let's try the process of elimination. Do you want to go and see Jimmy and Huguette? Or Johanne and Pierre?"

"No. I want to see new faces."

"How about going to Santa Cruz?"

"No."

"Do you want to go shopping?"

He's so sweet, he's ready for any sacrifice.

"No, Yves, I want to do something new. I've got to get out of here for a while. Why not visit a place we haven't been before? Escape.... Get away!"

"Listen, Diane, you've got something in mind, haven't you? I've got the feeling you're putting me on, you already know exactly what you want to do."

He's right. A bus trip has been organized by the recreation committee of Oak Creek Apartments, a two-day excursion to Reno, only seventy-two dollars all expenses paid. Yves must have read the announcement stuck up prominently on the bulletin board in the entrance to our building. In fact, I noticed a spark of interest in his eyes when I said, "Get away." He knows perfectly well what I'm driving at; after a short pause he says, "Do you think your doctor will let you get very far away from Stanford?"

Instead of replying I call the hospital. The medical team does authorize absences for a couple of days—they even encourage such initiatives because they're excellent for the patients' morale. "When you get there just give us a number where we can reach you, that's all."

Unfortunately I learn next that there's only one place left on the bus.

"Could we go by car?"

Yves opens the map. From San Francisco to Reno is 223 miles. Including the trip to San Francisco that makes four hours' driving. I pitch in by finding out about lodging: motels are only $20 a night and restaurant meals are real bargains.

So here we are on our way, our bags in the back, and Palo Alto disappearing behind us. On the road ahead everything's new and the landscape flies by. Quick, faster than the wind, catch up to time, pass it, leave it behind in our dust. Listen to the hum of the motor, lean back and enjoy the pleasure of moving effortlessly without moving your legs. Abandon routine. Forget the time, the date, and the telephone that refuses to ring. And if it does, imagine a mocking voice replying, "We've flown the coop, we're playing hookey from sickness. Too bad! We've just escaped!" Too bad for the birds, too. I left nectar for the humming-birds and peanuts for the jays—and now, my little friends, it's my turn to fly away.

To drive along and let your thoughts scatter is a way of tidying up your head, of airing your brain. It's letting go. And heading for Reno is like keeping your eye fixed on that little white ball without knowing where it will stop. Reno is known world-wide for its very liberal legislation on ultra-rapid marriage and divorce. But it's also one of the gambling capitals of the world, and that's what draws me there. What's a casino like? Who are these people who risk their fortunes on the chancy trajectory of a little ivory ball?

All in all, the people we see in the streets look very ordinary. They are simply dressed and the only sign of riches about them is their happy faces. It's a far cry from the beautiful women loaded with jewels and the superb gentlemen in evening clothes we've seen in French films. This is small-time Monte Carlo. The first surprise for Yves and me is that the little town is lit up like a Christmas tree. The streets are very lively and the parade never-ending. There are as many casinos as stores, all alight with high, flashing signs. And the traffic is as dense as rush hour, although it will soon be midnight and Yves is suggesting we should get some sleep. Not me! I insist. Have I already mentioned that he always gives in when it suits his purpose?

From the motel I telephone the hospital, leave a number where they can reach me, and then we go out again. We've decided not to spend more than twenty dollars apiece. But I'm lucky: the first silver dollar I put into a slot-machine comes back immediately, followed by two... three...four.... I stop counting—I've struck it rich! My first gamble is multiplied by forty. I try another dollar.... This time I win twenty. Sixty dollars in two tries! Fantastic, isn't it? I'm offered a glass of champagne. All the drinks are free. For that matter, everything's free. They calculate that any money lost on a drink or a meal will be raked in by a croupier or swallowed up by a slot-machine. Yves, who has sat down for five minutes at one of the gaming tables, tells me the magic hour has passed, for he's just lost five dollars. We go back to the hotel like a good little boy and girl, and I dream all night that I'm a millionaire.

Next morning I wake up feeling like breaking the bank. In the streets the same animation, day and night; the casinos never close. People play there, eat there, drink there twenty-four hours a day. I sit down in front of a machine, as sure of myself as a champion. Alas, this time it's a disaster. Even though I break my dollars up into small change, I lose everything I won yesterday, down to the last cent. So what? Time flew by. Gambling isn't all a question of winning and losing. I can play just to think about nothing else, play for the sake of playing. So I don't have any regrets about leaving the false luxury of those big rooms when Yves tells me, "Come on, Diane, we're going before I gamble away our gas money."

I make fun of him. I haven't lost a cent, I haven't even touched my twenty dollars. I'm proud of myself and happy to be back on the road. Once again I look out towards the horizon. Where to now? To the west where the sun is painting the mountains pink. Where do we come from? What were we doing in Reno? I don't know. Just killing time, really....

CHAPTER TWELVE

A Fairy Tale

February 7–10, 1984

On the telephone he tells me that his name is Jean-Paul Théorêt, that he's a member of the Laval Optimist Club, and that it's through them he heard my story. He's passing through San Francisco, and he'd like to meet Yves and me and get to know us, if we feel like it....

"Sure, it would be a pleasure."

"Do you want me to come up to Palo Alto?" he asks.

"Not at all. We'd much sooner come to San Francisco. That'll give us a chance to visit the city a second time."

"Okay. We can visit it together if you like. My wife is with me."

So he gives us the name and address of his hotel and we set off. The wheelchair is stored permanently in the trunk of the car, along with extra oxygen tanks, and all I have to do is take along my breathing tube in case I need it. Just a minute to touch up my make-up, and we're ready. An hour later we park the little Honda outside the impressive façade of the San Francisco Hotel.

"They must have come by plane," Yves says. "They certainly won't have a car. It's going to be embarrassing showing them around in our little old Swiss cheese."

I laugh. It's true the body of our Civic is rusted through in spots, but the motor is still good.

"Maybe we'd better do our sightseeing on foot," I say as we cross the thick carpet of the lobby.

The hotel may be sumptuous but the Théorêts are very simple people. They welcome us warmly and put us at ease right away. In a few words we sketch out a picture of our Californian life, tell them how we fill our days, how we keep our spirits up.

"And do you always have that smile?" Claudette asks. "How do you manage to be so courageous?"

I am always surprised to hear someone call "courage" what I would call an appetite for life.

"I do get demoralized sometimes, you know. But luckily Yves is here to cheer me up. And besides, I feel much better than when I came. I'm breathing better thanks to the eucalyptus."

"Eucalyptus?"

"Yes, those big trees with the leaves that smell so strong. No, that's right, you probably haven't seen them yet. Come on, we'll show you...."

"Let's eat first," says Jean-Paul.

So the four of us go to a little restaurant near the hotel. How good it is to have news from Quebec! We sit gossiping around the table for a long time. Now it's our turn to ask questions. What's the winter like this year? And the ski slopes? Lots of snow?

Did Jean-Paul notice a trace of nostalgia or sadness in my eyes? He replies a little evasively, "Listen, let's change the subject. What would you like to do today?"

"I told you this morning—visit San Francisco."

"Okay, let's go! I've rented a car for the day."

Yves gives me a relieved look. Jean-Paul gets up to pay the bill. We protest in vain.

"Listen," he cuts in, "let's get this clear. I'm inviting you today."

And he leads us to a line of monstrous cars and stops in front of one of them.

Call that a car? It's a twentieth-century Cinderella's coach. A limousine, long, white, complete with a chauffeur in uniform, TV, and bar. It even has a telephone. That'll be practical if my beeper decides to start sounding off. But I hope it won't get too excited today, because this afternoon I want to amble down Lombard Street, lose myself in the crowd in Chinatown, see the Golden Gate Bridge and Alcatraz. I want to stand at the top of the Coit Tower and see the city spread out at my feet. All the clichés, if you please. I want to take pictures of the pelicans on Fisherman's Wharf, those clumsy birds that you'd swear could never get off the ground. I want to mingle with the horde of tourists and imagine that I'm just one of them. And in fact that's what I do, sharing the carefree happiness of my three companions. That evening, after some hesitation, Jean-Paul adds an unforgettable souvenir to cap this delicious day. He undoes a chain he wears around his neck, takes a medal from it, and puts it into my hand. It's a gold cross with short, broad arms: on one side are three symbolic letters, on the other an image of the Pope.

"I got this medal in Rome. I hope it brings you luck."

I slip it onto the chain I wear round my neck.

"Thank you. I'll wear it as long as I live."

It's true. I've worn it ever since.

"How can we thank you both for this magic day?"

"It's simple. Get a good rest the two of you, because the day after tomorrow, Thursday, we've got a little surprise for you. We'll come by to get you about ten o'clock. That's not too early, is it?"

"No...."

"Good. Don't forget your pyjamas and your toothbrushes! And tell the hospital you'll be gone for a couple of days. It's getting late now, so good night...and see you Thursday!"

On Thursday the dream continues. We enjoy the luxurious comfort of the limousine again—the deep plush seats and the windows like giant TV screens looking out now on the sea,

71

immense and shimmering, now on the brown-layered rocks. We head south and for the first time go farther than Santa Cruz, to Monterey. We have supper at the Sardine Factory, with shark and octopus hors d'oeuvres. I taste them gingerly—I've got strong instincts of self-preservation!—but I'm hungry as a horse and gobble up my filet mignon. Everything's delicious, fabulous! We spend the night in a three-star hotel—the four-star one is full, which is a great disappointment for Jean-Paul. "Nothing's too good for you," he says.

He doesn't skimp on a single thing to make me happy.

The next morning we take the most beautiful road of the whole trip, Seventeen Mile Drive, between Pacific Grove and Mount Carmel. I won't even try to describe this famous highway playing hide-and-seek with the ocean; I just take some photos of the picturesque views, among them one of "The Lonely Cypress", the most photographed tree in the world. At least that's what our driver claims. He's been chauffeuring us now for three days and it's an experience full of surprises for him too. In ten years as a driver he's never seen the like: to be invited to sit down at table with the "boss" and try out his faulty French with a young woman who's twenty-six and condemned to death, yet goes on smiling and is happy simply to be alive—that doesn't happen every day.

"*J'espère rencontrer vous encore!*" he says awkwardly when he drops us at our apartment later that day.

"I hope so."

I do, but I doubt it. At least not in the same circumstances. Yves and I will certainly never have the means to afford a limousine and a chauffeur.

Outside the night is cold and filled with stars.

"Thank you again, Claudette and Jean-Paul!"

Who says fairy tales are made for children?

CHAPTER THIRTEEN

Valentine's Day

February 14, 1984

I had known it couldn't last. Yves had left, slamming the door, with me yelling after him, "That's right! Get out and don't come back!" I don't even remember what it was that got me into such a state. It must have been that damned television. What did it matter now? When I found myself alone I wanted to cry, I started to whimper, "If only he'd come back!" I stared at the door and sat there waiting absurdly for my gentle giant to walk through it and fall into my arms. I imagined his tears and his excuses and his words of tenderness. I'd definitely read too many Harlequin romances. But then it happened! The door did open very quietly, and my man came in. Only he didn't even look at me. He went straight over to one of the cupboards and took out two suitcases. His! And very calmly, without a word, without a look in my direction, he began going through his things.

"Yves, you're not going to leave in the middle of the night, are you? It's almost midnight...."

"...."

"Yves, I'm talking to you!"

"I'll leave tomorrow morning."

That's all I could get out of him. Next he put his bags down near the door, took a blanket off our bed, and stretched out on the sofa, completely dressed. Okay. I wasn't going to kneel down beside him and beg him to change his plans. Somewhat reassured by his presence, I left him, lay down alone on the big bed, and turned out the light. But there was no way I could get to sleep; I was too upset by our quarrel. We had got into the habit of yelling insults at each other more and more often. Something would have to be done. But what?

"Yves...are you asleep?"

No answer. Sulking as usual. That's his way—when he doesn't know what more to say, he stops cold. With me it's just the opposite, the less I know what to say, the more I carry on. And the more I get on his nerves, the more he clams up. It drives me crazy.

"Yves, are you asleep?"

Nothing. But he wasn't asleep. I could hear him perfectly well tossing and turning on the uncomfortable cushions of the sofa. I should have been thinking of something else, but what? Every time I closed my eyes the image of Debbie Mora sprang up. I kept seeing her as she was when she came to visit us with two of her children: leaning over one of them—the youngest, Norman, I think—and smiling at him exactly the way she did right here in the studio. It's stupid the images that remain with you even after people are gone, little scenes cut off from everyday life. I can't remember why Debbie was leaning over her son like that— maybe it was just to tie up his shoe or push his hair out of his eyes. But she was smiling at him, and I caught such a feeling of closeness between them in that instant that I immediately felt indiscreet to be watching. For a second, one tiny second, I envied them this closeness.

Since then, each time I think of Debbie it isn't as the gracious hostess of the Thanksgiving dinner but as the mother reaching out tenderly to her son, with a gesture so commonplace that I've forgotten what it was. And I couldn't help thinking, playing back that fragment of film as I lay in the darkness, that the incident would never be repeated except in my memory. It was all over. Debbie would never smile at Norman again. He would never again read that generous expression of love in his mother's face. Debbie was dead and nobody could exchange anything with her. This idea revolted and humiliated me at the same time. Every time I looked inside my head at all seriously, I ran up against this tender image with the words "The End" written across it. It was unjust. Who has the right to interrupt happiness?

Nobody, absolutely nobody has a suitable answer to that question. But instead of admitting my helplessness, instead of resigning myself, I nourished my sense of revolt. It must have been for that reason that I became more insufferable every day. At the least pretext I would bury Yves in reproaches and wear myself out hurling insults at him. I exaggerated his clumsiness. I was right in the thick of this self-analysis, stretched out in the dark, when I felt somebody beside me. It was Yves, lying on top of the covers a good distance away. From sheer habit I had left his place empty and was over on my own side of the bed. I must admit I felt a flush of triumph knowing he was there, as though he'd brought me proof of his attachment. But I wasn't going to accept his forgiving me for my nagging. He had taken the first step, fine! That meant he felt he had something to reproach himself with. So it was up to him to say the first words.

It was a long wait because Yves is as proud as I am stubborn. I lay still while he turned restlessly from one side to the other, heaving sighs of impatience. Once he got up to go to the bathroom, another time to get undressed. Then he slipped in between the sheets. I must admit that at that moment I almost gave in; I had to grip my side of the bed solidly to avoid rolling over to him. At last he spoke:

"Diane, I know very well you're not asleep...."

"..."

"...so for once listen to me and try not to interrupt...."

I listened, but that's all. I didn't say a word. Even when he flatly accused me of being selfish and unjust I held my peace. Of course I was boiling inside—you don't take all that truth on the chin without reacting. As usual I bit my nails while waiting for him to stop treating me like some kind of frustrated, ungrateful egoist. But he had a lot on his chest. To listen to him you'd think I was a capricious little girl, manipulative, thankless, and incapable of generosity. According to him, nothing could justify my spoilt-brat behaviour, above all not my illness. That was too easy. No, things couldn't go on like this and there was only one solution.

Obviously, he was right. There was only one solution, we would have to part. We couldn't go on destroying each other with insults and this kind of idiotic behaviour. But I dreaded a separation and refused to admit that it had become inevitable. Which prompted me to cry out, despite myself:

"I can't, Yves! I *won't*."

"But why, Diane? Why don't you want to move?"

"...Move?"

"Why yes, it's the only solution. We have to find a bigger apartment where we won't be in each other's hair twenty-four hours a day. An apartment where there's an extra room so we can each spend some time alone.... But, Diane, what's so funny about that? What are you laughing at?"

Because it was true, I'd broken out in a nervous laugh that came issuing from my mouth like a long, jumpy, frantic ribbon of irrepressible sound—a joyous cascade of pure laughter that shook my whole body and freed me of all hang-ups, fears, and anguish. A laugh that, alas, didn't prove to be very contagious.

"Is that all you can find to say?"

No, of course not. I finally found something to say. I think I even talked my head off a good part of the night. I made plans. We'd find a way to get out of the lease. If that turned out to be difficult, I'd get a letter from Dr. Jamieson saying that my state of health required a larger apartment. Yes, that's right, and with an extra room. We'd be able to find a more suitable place off campus. Several patients lived at Mountain View, a little industrial town not too far from the hospital. After all, we only

had to be within an hour's drive of Stanford. Tomorrow I'd buy
the papers and start to go through the classifieds.

"You'll see, Yves, I'll find something."

"We'll find something."

So that's how we decided to move. Our apartment manager
sounded impressed by my medical excuse. He even offered us
one of his two-room studios, a real bargain, $200 off the regular
price. How much would that be? Just $1,200 with no extras. A
bargain? Thanks very much, we'll look somewhere else. It was
at Mountain View that we began our search. I knew that in a
town less well known than Palo Alto we'd have a better chance
of finding something in our range. After several disappointing
visits we found ourselves in a large, sunny apartment. Yves took
a quick look in the kitchen and came out saying, "It's perfect,
Diane—we don't have to look any further."

"What? But we haven't even seen it yet!"

I made my way into the living room. There were wide French
doors opening out onto quite a big balcony, and in the distance,
over the roofs of the buildings opposite, there was a superb view
of the mountains.

"That's west, Yves. Can you imagine! We'll see the sunset
every day. And look, the living room is big enough to have a
dinette in that corner. And listen—there are birds too, we'll be
able to set up our feeder. Do you think there'll be humming-
birds? Oh, Yves, come and see the bedroom! And the bathroom's
right beside it.... Practical, eh?"

"Right! Now come and see the kitchen," he said impatiently.

"Well, what's so extraordinary about it?"

I really didn't see. There were all the usual appliances, the
stove, the fridge, the dishwasher....

"A dishwasher, Diane! Don't you know I've been dreaming
of one every day, at that certain time just after dinner?"

Really! Ever since he took up cooking he's been developing
the mentality of a housewife. It's high time he got some help
from these domestic robots, or I wonder what will become of his
intellectual capacities. He obviously needs some rest.

That's why next morning, bubbling over with good intentions, I did my best to get rid of him. Right after the dishes I sent him out of the house.

"Yves, haven't you got any errands to do?"

"No."

"You know, you've only got a few days left to look at the fancy cars of all those Stanford doctors. Exactly a week from today we'll have changed neighbourhoods. Why don't you go out and count the BMWs and Rolls-Royces and Ferraris on Willow Road?"

"You'd think you were trying to get rid of me.... Have you got something special in mind?"

"No, nothing in particular. Some overdue letters to write and that painting to finish for the Théorêts."

"Is that all?"

"It's enough, isn't it? You know I concentrate better when I'm alone."

"Okay, I'll go for a walk."

He really seemed to suspect something. He took forever to trim his moustache, while I thrummed the table impatiently.

"Yves, aren't you ready to leave yet?"

"Just remember, sweetheart, that this time it's *you* telling me to get out."

Of course he was alluding to our spat the other night. Okay, he asked for it.

"And wasn't it you, darling, who came and climbed back into bed with me?"

"I didn't like to mention it, dear, but you can't imagine how uncomfortable those sofa cushions are."

"*Liar!*"

I was furious and slammed the door after him. So he refused to admit he stayed because he loved me. Well, I'd get my revenge! He had his nerve! He was the envy of hundreds of Québécois for being the privileged companion of that charming Diane Hébert, and he was a monster of arrogance and ingratitude. He'd find out this very day that his partner had a heart of gold.

I found everything I needed in the kitchen. In a great deal more time than it takes to tell, I'd made two square shapes, covered one with icing, and stuck the other on top. This precision work, which required much more dexterity than culinary talent, made me feel good. I felt like a great surgeon matching auricles and ventricles. Finally, to add to the fun, I mixed colouring into two other parts of the icing and used them to decorate my Valentine's present. It was a *chef d'oeuvre*!

When Yves came back there was a heart-shaped cake on the table and a lot of dirty dishes in the sink. He didn't complain. He washed and dried them all without a word. He also prepared supper, spaghetti for a change. He seemed to appreciate my dessert, but I know it was my talent as a decorator rather than my skill as a cook that surprised him most. Because in pretty pink letters on top of the cake I had traced out three words I hadn't said for too long a time: "I Love You."

CHAPTER FOURTEEN

Bad Dream

March 21, 1984

8:15 p.m.

We've just moved into our new apartment and we're as excited
as kids. Yves puts a box down in the middle of the rug in the
living room and begins to unpack it.

"I'm going to install it right now," he says.

"Okay, I'll help. What do we need, a screwdriver?"

"Yes, and the small pliers. And bring your dictionary—the
instructions are in English."

"I'll get them."

We've just bought a VCR. It's the latest addition to our
furnishings, which have increased considerably since we moved:
we now have some chairs, a lot more house plants, an aquarium,
and twenty fish. Naturally that meant extra expenditures, but the
Laval Optimist Club hasn't objected. The money the Foundation
has raised is ample to see us comfortably furnished. It isn't a
question of spending frivolously but of improving our lifestyle
within reason.

So we made that last purchase with a clear conscience. The increased living space in our new place has made us more sedentary. Now our old studio seems like a temporary perch, while this place is getting more and more like a place we'd really like to live in. It seems that we've relaxed about putting down roots in California, or have at least consented to become residents here for as long as necessary. With the VCR we can rent films, record some good programs, and above all we can finally watch the tapes my parents have been saving for our return. Now, whenever we want we can treat ourselves to the illusion that we're back home looking at a Quebec TV screen. I must call Maman tonight and ask her to send us the cassettes. Coincidentally the telephone rings. It's 8:30.

"Have you got them?" asks Yves.

"What?"

"The small pliers!"

"Yes, but just a minute, let me get the phone first.... *Allo, oui!*"

A man's voice tells me in English that he is calling from the Stanford Hospital and that he is Dr. McGregor. I don't know this doctor. I've never heard his name before.

"Mrs. Hébert? You have to come to the hospital as quickly as possible. We have a potential donor for you."

I translate simultaneously in my head. This doctor whom I don't even know is telling me I have a donor. Somehow I don't believe him. Either he's crazy, I think instinctively, or it's a joke.

"You're trying to trick me. Is this some kind of a prank?"

But the gentleman seems very put out by the suggestion that I could take him for a prankster. He repeats his piece twice more and insists that I come *immediately*. I hang up. Yves is looking at me.

"What is it, Diane, a wrong number?"

"No, it's a joke...."

"What do you mean?"

"Do you know a Dr. McGregor?"

"No. What did he say?"

"He claims he has a donor. I wonder who would play a trick like that."

"But Diane...."

"Do you think it could be Chuck? But this so-called doctor had a very British accent."

Yves is on his feet now, very nervous.

"Diane, maybe it's not a joke. Call the hospital back right away."

"Should I?"

It's no joke. Dr. McGregor belongs to the Stanford medical team and is waiting for me impatiently. At least, that's what they say at the other end of the line. I still can't believe it. Why do they have to choose such an impossible time?

"I don't want to go, Yves!"

"Are you crazy or what?"

"And what if I don't make it through the operation? What if I don't get out alive? I've been feeling so much better lately, maybe I don't need a transplant...."

"Listen, you're feeling better because you're resting more, because I've been doing everything for you. But you know perfectly well that the least little effort tires you and you're always out of breath. Come on, you can't tell me you're not sick."

He's right. I don't talk easily about my weaknesses or pains. Yves knows I resist complaining and self-pity with all my strength. What good would it do, anyway? Now Yves has followed me into the bedroom.

"Okay, I'll get ready," I say without enthusiasm. "Hand me down the big suitcase, the one on the top shelf there. What should I take with me? A blouse, a sweater—which one, the pink or the blue? Or both of them?"

Yves is furious.

"You're not going on a trip, Diane. Take as little as possible. If you need anything, I'll bring it. Come on, there's no time to lose."

I take my make-up kit and some toilet articles just the same, and make sure I've got my address book and something to write with. I take a last look around the apartment and at the new VCR....

"You'll get it hooked up while I'm gone?"

"Sure, sure. Come on!"

"Don't forget the plants and the fish. And the birds, Yves—promise you'll feed them?"

There are tears in my eyes.

"I won't forget, Diane. Come on now, hurry."

8:45 p.m.

We're driving on the superhighway, passing everyone. Yves's hands are glued to the wheel, his eyes are fixed on the road, we're gobbling up the miles. The speed is intoxicating, I'm getting feverish. Everything seems unreal, lights jumping at us out of the darkness. Am I dreaming? Is it me in this race against death, or is it a dream?

9:00 p.m.

We're at the hospital. Yves has broken all the records; it's taken him fifteen minutes to cover a distance that usually takes more than half an hour. Here I am. I'm ready! But where are the doctors? There's not a single man in white in sight, only a receptionist who has obviously never had to deal with a transplant case before. Anyway, there's no urgency. We know that at Stanford this kind of operation is only performed in the daytime, from 6:00 a.m. on. Is it so the surgeons have better light, or just so they get a good night's sleep? It's probably just the Stanford custom and it has proved effective—so there's no question of arguing with the practice, even if it means the patient is plunged into agonies of interminable waiting. I'm getting impatient. I'd at least like to go up to my room. Why do they keep me twiddling my thumbs here? I fill out the usual forms and hand them back to the receptionist, who assures me that someone will be along to get me....

"Yves, do you think I should call my parents?"

"Not now, Diane, wait a little while longer."

Wait...? A little while! Longer?

10:07 p.m.

A young orderly tells us to follow him. None too soon. Second floor, a double room opposite the nurses' station. I can slip on a cardigan and sit on my bed. At last Dr. McGregor shows up. He doesn't look at all like a prankster: he's thin, fortyish, with thinning blond hair, lively, nervous, efficient, like most of the doctors here in fact. He welcomes me and they begin the examinations. I'm not dreaming after all. Nurses come and go. Blood samples, X-rays—it seems pretty real to me. They send for an interpreter to translate something for me, an important paper I have to sign. I agree to accept the risks and consequences of the operation. If only they knew! Do they have no inkling that I'd sign their papers with my eyes closed? I know all too well that this transplant is my one chance of survival. Can they take photos too? As many as they want, I've nothing to hide. I'm even interested to find out how they go about making the mysterious substitution.

11:19 p.m.

They've brought me vitamin K, which acts as an anti-coagulant, and a small dose of cyclosporin. That's an anti-rejection drug; it's the magic potion for transplant patients. Since its discovery the success rate has climbed to 80 per cent. Chuck, who has just come in, encourages me to swallow it. "You'll get used to it, you'll see. In a few days you'll have cheeks like a chipmunk." Yes, I know. My face will be swollen and my cheeks will be covered with fuzz—those are the side-effects, I've heard about them. But what difference does that make since I'll really be living again, able to walk without being short of breath, to run like a girl. I swallow it down making a bad face. Ugh! It tastes like cod liver oil. Chuck smiles at me. He seems sincerely glad my turn has come. "You won't have to wait any more," he says. He knows that's the most difficult part. How right he is; it's still only 11:19 by my watch. I cast a discreet glance at the telephone. Yves has been watching:

"Not just yet, Diane!"

An orderly comes in and starts to pull the curtains around my bed. He wants to shave me. It seems that here they shave their patients from neck to knee. That's a bit much, isn't it?

"I don't want it!"

He insists. I refuse.

"You can do it tomorrow morning! My hair will grow during the night, can't you see? Go shave the donor instead."

I don't know if he understands, but he goes away. Does he really go to shave the donor? For that matter, where is the donor? Yves thinks he heard that the donor was taken to a Los Angeles hospital and then flown here by helicopter. Killed in a traffic accident, no doubt. Clinically dead, zero chance of survival, organs kept alive artificially. Is it a woman, a man, or a child? I don't know and I never will. It's a closely guarded secret and for good reason—there are all kinds of stories going around. There's the one about the woman who consented to let her dead husband's organs be used and finally fell in love with the recipient. She claimed her husband's heart still beat for her! As if everyone doesn't know that the seat of love is the brain! I know it's less poetic to say, "My brain cogitates for you," than "My heart beats for you," but it's strange, just the same, to see what a lot people always unload on the heart. Yes, I know, I'm the first to be sucked in. Didn't I spend a whole afternoon cutting a cake into the shape of an idealized heart? Would it ever have occurred to me to make it the shape of a pump?

"Yves, tell me that it's not a dream, that I'm not delirious."

"You're not dreaming, Diane, but you do look tired. If you like, Chuck and I could leave."

"No, don't go! Stay! Don't leave me alone!"

Anyway, people keep coming and going as though the room were a railway station. There, another nurse, another little pill. What is it this time, more medication? No, a tranquillizer. As if I needed one. Do I have to go to sleep?

"How do you expect me to sleep? Tomorrow I'm going to be born again and you're asking me to sleep?"

Chuck translates for the nurse and she laughs. He must have got it mixed up. Chuck is nice, and so funny, too. Not like Yves who is as serious as an owl and can't stop looking at his watch and the phone.

12:01 a.m.

It's not morning yet in Montreal, but what difference does that make? I've got to call my parents. They have to know. Too bad if I wake them up.

"Allo, Maman?"

Her voice is thick with sleep. She cries, laughs, puts Papa on, goes on talking behind him, takes the phone again, gives it back to Papa. They're happy, more excited than I am. I know they won't be able to go back to sleep now and won't be able to wait to tell the others. That's okay. For everyone except Isabelle. I haven't the right to interrupt her sleep. Because if by chance I didn't wake up, if by chance everything turned out wrong....

Yves is calling his parents. He has his usual dispassionate look, but his voice betrays his emotion. I want to talk to them.

"Yes, that's right, tomorrow morning—that is, in a few hours. It's hard waiting...."

"Be brave, Diane, we'll be thinking of you."

"Thanks. Okay, here's Yves again...."

12:20 a.m.

Everything has quieted down now. I can feel sleep stealing over me. My head is heavy and my eyes close by themselves. I suppose it's just a dream and I'm going to wake up in my own bed.

"Yves, are you there?"

"Yes."

"And Chuck?"

"He's here too. Are you tired? You seem sleepy."

"No. I just prefer keeping my eyes shut. What time is it?"

LA PRESSE

How could I guess that one day I'd make the front page of the morning papers because I had an incurable disease?

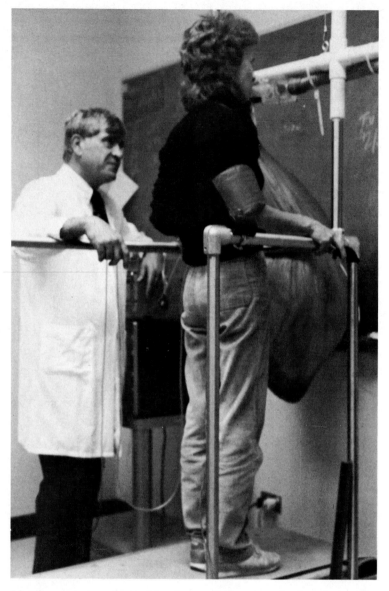

I finally manage to understand that these preliminary examinations don't require any hospitalization. (Shown here is a respiratory test conducted by Dr. James Theodore of the University of Stanford Medical Center.)

Yves looks after me, cares for me like a baby, does the housework and the dishes. Isn't his continual presence by my side a tangible proof of his tenderness for me?

The day after his second heart-lung transplant, Chuck was awake and smiling; three weeks later he was drinking wine with his hospital meals. Here he is a few days after the operation.

I always breathe better when mail comes from Quebec; it's like a strong wind of love reaching me. I try to find unusual ways to thank the people who write to me.

Andrea Matsushima (front) died on Jan. 9, 1985, right after her transplant. Left of me, Jo Ann Zulaica had her first transplant on April 10, 1985, and is waiting for a second because of a viral infection. Right of me, Judy Holden had her transplant on July 25, 1984, and is in perfect health; Gayle Reedy died on Nov. 13, 1984, a week after his operation; Judy Skidmore died in May 1986 while waiting for her transplant; John Tedeschi died on May 23, 1985, eleven months after his transplant; Donna Isom withdrew from the program; Stephen Epstein died before receiving his transplant.

I'm coming back to this city and this house after being away two years almost to the day, and nothing seems to have altered.

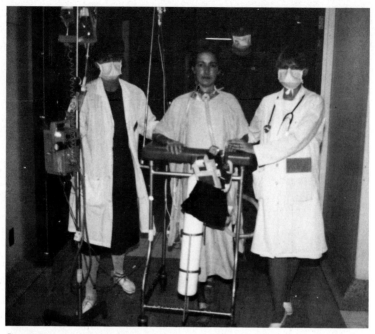

Just getting up and standing seems to be an act of pure masochism. It feels as though my bones are fractured into thousands of little pieces that threaten to crumble as soon as I want to make them move.

Today I've come to tell the people of Quebec that they were right to believe in me. I deserved their confidence. I'm here today as proof that I've won.

In Montreal I even went dancing, as I'd promised I would.

People listen to me now with real fervour, and I sometimes have the impression, when I'm speaking into a microphone or before an audience, that they're hanging on my words. I feel they're ready to follow me.

"Twenty past twelve."

"Still? Are you sure?"

"Yes. Go to sleep now."

No, it's impossible to sleep in this room. Two doctors come in and close the door behind them. They're both in dressing gowns. The biggest one has a screwdriver in his hand, the other the small pliers. They approach the bed smiling. They don't look like bad men. They tell me in French that they're making a television program. It's only then that I recognize them as Réal and Pierre from Radio-Canada. Next they tell me that the transplant operation was a success and that it has been entirely filmed from the inside. Sure enough, they've installed a video camera on my chest. Yet I feel no weight and no pain. On the contrary, I feel extremely well. "It's funny," I say, "I didn't feel a thing." "That's because you were asleep," says Réal. "It's because you were dreaming," says Pierre.

Yes, I was sleeping. I know I was dreaming because now I've opened my eyes. Two men *are* leaning over me. This time I recognize them right away. The big one is Yves, the other is Dr. McGregor. They don't look particularly happy to see me smiling. They look worried. I must reassure them, explain to them that I feel better now, that everything is all over. I look the doctor in the eyes and, still smiling, ask:

"It's all done, doctor?"

"No, Diane...."

What do you mean, no? I look around me. No tubes, no respirator, I'm not in intensive care, I'm in the same room I was in earlier. Through the window the sky is getting light; it will soon be daybreak. It's 5:37. All right, just another hour to wait but...why are they looking at me like that?

"The donor is too big."

"What? What's he saying, Yves? The donor's too big? This can't be happening to me!"

"But it's true, Diane."

"We're sorry, Mrs. Hébert."

"*Sorry?* You *are* a joker! I told you yesterday it was a joke!"

87

I wonder where I find the words? I didn't know I knew so many swearwords in English. They pour out of me like a jet of boiling water. Yves doesn't know where to look.

I go on in French:

"*C'est une vraie bande de fous, Yves.* They should be locked up. You don't do things like that! *Trop gros! Trop gros!* Get that! They might have taken some measurements, no? Didn't they know I was small?"

"The information they sent by telephone was very sketchy. They thought the organs would match. It's a mistake, Diane...."

"They shouldn't make mistakes. Don't they know this kind of false alarm is practically impossible to bear? Come on, Yves, let's get out of here. I don't want to stay one second more in this hospital full of incompetent idiots. They made a fool of me. I don't want to see them again! Ever!"

Yves unlocks the door. The apartment is exactly the way we left it yesterday. Nothing has moved except the fish, who go on swimming back and forth in their glass house. Do fish talk? Do they cry out silently when they open their mouths? Before I left the hospital I learned that the heart and lungs that were destined for me would be transplanted to the chest of Roberta Kmetz. She's scarcely bigger than I am. Roberta's only been waiting since January, but she was hospitalized last week. She's seriously ill. According to the doctors she's only got a few more days to live. I can't reasonably hold anything against her. Her lucky day has come. Is it her fault that they thought the donor would do for me? No. But this helps me understand all those efforts on the part of the medical team to avoid competition between recipients. Cases like this could easily stir up hatred and kill friendships....

A few minutes ago I called the hospital to apologize. I was unfair, my feelings of revolt swamped whatever good sense I had left. For now I have only one desire, one wish, one need: to slip between the sheets and sleep. The VCR still stands there half unpacked. Maybe we can rewind and pretend nothing happened, sleep until eight and wake up believing this whole incident, this little fragment of time, was nothing after all but a bad dream.

CHAPTER FIFTEEN

Signs of Life

April 25, 1984

A few days ago, under the shade of a eucalyptus, I read *The Gift of Life*, the news bulletin put out by the patients waiting for heart-lung transplants.

"Listen to this, Yves. Every year between 12,000 and 27,000 people are declared clinically dead in the U.S., but in 1983 only 2,500 were organ donors. Discouraging figures, eh?"

"Yes and no, Diane. It proves your chances could get better...."

"That's true. Lots of people are afraid to leave their bodies to science. There must be a way to explain to them, to make them understand that this gift—this legacy of theirs—could save other human lives."

"Yes, but how?"

"They have to be encouraged to be more generous. They have to get rid of this ridiculous fear. I've got an idea, Yves. During Organ Donor Week we could hold a press conference and invite lots of people.... Do you think Marguerite Brown would be willing to help?"

"Maybe."

Marguerite Brown is program coordinator for transplants at Stanford. She's been working here for ten years and knows the subject inside out. Yet she seemed somewhat reluctant about the idea of a campaign to raise public awareness. Heart-lung transplants are relatively recent and still at the experimental stage, so it seemed premature to her to run a publicity campaign and lead a lot of people to believe in this operation as a sort of guarantee of survival. And besides, she was reluctant to solicit such an intimate gift from people. It's not a question of asking for organs the way you'd ask for money, even if the cause is urgent. The problem is delicate and has to be treated with extreme care. After expressing these reservations, this wise and subtle woman agreed to present a slide show, a short history of transplant operations. Yves and I looked after the rest: we got the use of a room in the apartment building we live in, we drew up an announcement of the event, and Yves has left photocopies in five hundred mailboxes in the neighbourhood.

I'm glad to be active and to have an opportunity to work at last—whatever they say, it's not normal to be on holiday all your life. All the little jobs connected with the organization of this evening's event have got my energy perking again. I feel full of enthusiasm and ideas. I've got things worked out so the presentation can reach people back home too. We've borrowed a video camera, and if Yves turns out to be a good cameraman we'll send our "made for TV" film to Quebec. That way our friends and supporters will be able to see our new home, our new friends here, the landscape we live in, and above all Marguerite Brown's slide show. It's really fun to be a producer, and I discover that work like this is just play. Yves is having a great time too. Together we've worked out the general theme and have begun to film our surroundings.

Is it spring that fills us with life and makes the air so good to breathe? Or is it another rebirth that has made us so joyous? The day before yesterday, the first day of Organ Donor Week, John Tedeschi received a new heart and lungs. It's the fourth transplant since we arrived. He had been waiting only two months.

"Another man," I say to Yves.

"What about Roberta?"

"Sure, Roberta, okay, but she got them instead of me...."

"Diane, you'd think you held that against her."

"No, Yves, I just think she's lucky. I've got a right to think she's lucky, haven't I?"

For that matter, Roberta is getting along famously. She just feels a little uneasy—as if she has stolen something from me. I've tried to reason with her, but she feels guilty. I've told her that I'd probably be dead if they'd put those lungs and heart in me. And she would be too, for not getting them. She's alive...and me too! What else matters?

So I'm doubly happy for Roberta and John. They're lucky to be reborn at a time when nature is bursting into bloom all around us. It's the first time I've seen California so green and flowery. Is it spring that makes life so succulent, so full of promise? It seems there's a surge of sap impatiently boiling away somewhere inside the planet, as if a giant child were struggling to be born. The proof is that yesterday the earth shook. Yves and I were sitting in a corner of our kitchenette drinking 7-Up and chatting quietly. Suddenly our glasses began to clink together, the table started to shake, and the lamp above our heads began swinging gently along with the hanging plants. I didn't even have time to be afraid. By the time we realized we were having our first earthquake, it was already over. The bubbles went on rising in our soft drinks, and you could still hear the reassuring gurgle of the aquarium. It was over. A little shock a few seconds long and nothing more. Was it at that moment I thought that death ought to come so quickly? A second's astonishment, then nothing. Not even time to know what was happening. That wouldn't be so terrible!

We didn't have any damage. Around us, however, chests of drawers emptied their contents on the floor, walls fell, houses were knocked down. No fatalities. Just the planet giving a kick to let humans know it was really alive. A little warning to tell us we're all mortal and we'd better hurry out and enjoy the spring.

Spring is a flock of ducklings we fed as usual this morning. There are seven of them puddling around in the pond doing their aquatic ballet, much less graceful than comic. You can't help laughing at them. Then after lunch we went to see John Tedeschi at the hospital. I filmed him through the window of intensive care. Just two days after the operation and he was sitting up in bed making friendly signs to us. He pointed to his puffy cheeks and smiled. Yves asked if he could go in to see him; he had to get dressed up in a sterilized gown. He looked like a big microbe. Afterwards we put the finishing touches on our preparation for tonight: we bought some snacks and got extra chairs in case of overflow.

Unfortunately only about thirty people came. Some neighbours from the apartment, our friends, and the usual members of our meetings. Could it be that life only interests those who risk losing it, or who fear for those dear to them? It's possible.

"It's because it's spring, Yves. It's too nice outside to sit locked up in a room."

"It's true, we should have had the meeting out under the stars."

"That wouldn't have been enough to draw a crowd. No, I think we should have shown something more than tables and statistics and photos of transplants."

"But it was very interesting, Diane; I learned things I didn't know."

"Me too, but I think the public we're trying to reach would have been more impressed with other images."

"What, for instance?"

"I don't know yet. Maybe a film would have been more appropriate. Yes, a film showing a person who has pulmonary hypertension who talks about the progress of the disease, the long wait, and then the rebirth."

"I can see you coming from a long way off, Diane, but I warn you, I have no talent as a filmmaker. I think the film we tried to make is a complete failure."

"Well, you were holding the camera crooked! You could at least have kept things in the middle."

"You're right, it was my fault. And it's spring that's to blame. What next? You're not going to blame the whole world just because you're disappointed?"

"Disappointed? Who, me? Well, for once you've got it wrong. I'm not disappointed. It's true I worked very hard for this show—I worked so hard I forgot to remember."

"To remember what?"

"To remember that a year ago I had no idea whether I'd see another springtime or not. And it's here, Yves! The crickets have begun to sing again, and I'm alive! That's what I have to tell the world, Yves, that life is so wonderful you mustn't ever let it slip away."

CHAPTER SIXTEEN

A Question of Faith

June 4, 1984

It's too much—I'll never be able to answer all these letters. They're piled up beside my computer and the pile goes on growing every day. It may sound as though I'm complaining but in reality there's nothing I like better than the postman's ring. It's true! I call him my Santa Claus. Ever since we've been in Mountain View not a day has gone by without his bringing us mail. And when I say mail I also mean parcels. Things keep pouring in: Bibles, holy images, scapulars, medals, postcards, photos, newspaper clippings, trinkets in the shape of flowers or birds or hearts, knitted slippers, sweaters, cassettes, books, and widely varying sums of money. In Palo Alto during January and February the people of Quebec had already sent me numerous proofs of their generosity. But here at Mountain View the month of May beat all records: 151 letters in all, 104 in the first week.

I owe this abundance to Quebec journalists who published the story of my cancelled operation on page one. The tale of my disappointed hopes touched many hearts. "Don't let it get you down." "Keep on going." "Keep your courage up." "Never give up." "Pray." The messages came from everywhere. Many of my correspondents suggested the names of patron saints whose favour I might solicit. Yves makes fun of all the printed prayers that accompany the letters, prayers to Saint Jude or Sainte Eulalie, not forgetting Our Lady of Holy Hope.

"At this rate you won't know which saint to pray to!"

"Don't laugh, Yves. You ought to respect these people who still trust in someone. It doesn't matter who it is they believe in."

"And you, do you believe?"

"Yes. I believe in my Big Pal in the sky. Call him the Ineffable, the Divine Power, the Creator, or the Good Lord, it's all the same thing. I know it gets on your nerves terribly to think I have an invisible Big Pal in the sky."

You'd think he was jealous, you'd think he held it against me that I had some sort of secret line to the beyond, as if he were afraid a rival was taking his place. Yet he can hardly say I overindulge this funny friendship of mine. It's just that at night I like to be able to talk to someone before going to sleep without it turning into a squabble. This friend doesn't answer back. He doesn't reproach me for my impatience or my hasty words; he listens; he soothes me....

"He doesn't quarrel with me!"

"Yes, but he doesn't answer either."

"It's because I don't ask him for anything. I'm not sure he wants to give me a new heart or a new pair of lungs. Maybe he has other plans for me. It's his decision, understand?"

"You seem to be pretty docile with him!"

"I trust him because he doesn't judge me. That's what friendship is, isn't it? He lets me do what I want, so I let him decide for me. And even if I don't know what 'his will' is, I respect it because he respects me."

"It's all in your head. You're inventing someone to reassure you."

"No, I'm not inventing someone, or else millions of us are inventing him. And even if I am talking to myself, supposing you're right—what difference does that make to you if it makes me stronger?"

"It's all a bunch of old wives' tales...."

"You're dead wrong! Lots of men write to me about their faith too."

Yves doesn't reply. What can he add anyway? He has to admit that these hundreds of people supporting me help as much as he does to keep my hope alive. And that bothers him a little, not to be the only one helping me through this ordeal.... Or rather, to be the only one who has to put up with my bad character. But he can't deny that on this score I've improved vastly. It's true— with that strong wind of affection blowing my way from Quebec, forcing me to stand up straight and look to the future, my morale is high and I've got wind in my sails. All that helps keep my little boat moving. And during the first week in May it was truly speeding along. It was Yves's boat that had sprung a leak.

So I took advantage of a visit from Isabelle and my parents to turn him loose and give him a holiday. He was very happy to spend ten days in Montreal. He hadn't seen his own parents for six months, and he missed them. He looked up some old pals of his and they went up to the Laurentians. As for me, I took my visitors on a tour with Ken and Dorothy in their mobile home. We went all the way to Monterey and Carmel. Isabelle was in seventh heaven. We spent lots of time feeding the squirrels in a big park. I think she loves animals as much as I do. On the way back Ken decided to spend the night in a campground beside the ocean. There were many fishermen and an old wrecked ship we could explore. Isabelle and I collected shells and stones until dusk.

"Look, Maman, here's one that looks like a heart."

She was holding up a flat round stone.

"Here, I'll give it to you because yours is no good any more."

"Thank you, Isabelle."

"When are you going to get your new little heart, Maman?"

"I don't know, *ma petite*."

"And afterwards, when you've got it, will you come back to your big house? It's so small here...."

"Yes, it's too small. Things will be better back home.... Look, a starfish!"

She's full of wonder, this child of mine, and she's passionately fond of nature, like me. The next day we built sand castles and the rest of the time passed like a dream. This visit sped by like the one before, and the shock of separation brought tears to my eyes again, a side-effect of such intense happiness.

Luckily, my man came back in great shape with a host of anecdotes to tell, among them the story of how the frankfurters got through customs. Yes, I'd asked Yves to do a few errands for me in Montreal, to get me some exotic products like, well, hot dogs. I know they exist in California, but they're inedible. Anyway, that's what I think, and Yves shared my opinion enough to go along with my whim. So before leaving Montreal he wrapped up several packages of wieners in newspaper and sealed the whole thing with black plastic tape so it wouldn't leak in the suitcase. The customs' officer became immediately suspicious of this young bozo and his casual manner.

"What's in the suitcase?" my courier was asked.

Without listening to the reply, the officer opened it and, sure he had unearthed a kilo of heroin, pointed at the innocent package.

"Hold it! Don't move!"

My immovable friend didn't move.

"They're hot dogs," he felt prompted to explain.

Obviously a zealous customs officer is hardly going to believe "a French-Canadian with a German name living in California." Other skeptical officials arrived and in turn sniffed the package like hungry dogs.

"You should have seen their faces when I unwrapped the frankfurters...."

"Did they go on searching you?"

"Not at all. They saw their mistake and excused themselves. They were very polite. They even gave me advice on how to avoid trouble next time."

"Advice?"

"Yes, they told me I should get a temporary resident's visa and bring letters from the bank and the doctors."

"So you told them my story. You see how useful I can be—a real password. You know, I'm beginning to get famous. Just look at all the mail I've got since you left."

Yves didn't react. Ordinarily, when I turn everything around to my credit, it gets his goat. But the little trip did him good. He's rediscovered his angelic patience. I think this separation was good for both of us; now we'll love each other better and tone down our eternal squabbling.

"Diane, I'm glad to be back. I've fallen seriously in love with California."

"What do you mean, California? Don't you love me first?"

"Yes, you too. But not more than California. Let's say it's not the same kind of feeling."

"Well, if that's it, if I have a rival, you'll have to put up with a rival too."

"Who?"

"My Big Pal in the sky."

"You're not going to start that again?"

"But it's the same kind of thing, isn't it?"

"If you want...."

"Then you admit he exists?"

Yves scratches his head. He looks as if he's making a big effort to say, "Well, okay, if you believe it...."

CHAPTER SEVENTEEN

Three Reasons for Hope

July 25, 1984

Towards the end of April Yves had a call from Chuck. There was nothing very surprising in that; they had become good friends and sometimes saw each other "man to man". But this time Yves was surprised by Chuck's request for someone to drive him to the hospital. "Stanford's Number Two" was used to managing on his own, especially for visits to the medical centre.

"Just go on with your painting," said Yves, seeing me absorbed at my easel.

That very morning I had begun a little summer landscape that was giving me a lot of pleasure. The sky was especially satisfactory; I'd found a way of making it transparent the way a California sky really is. I didn't feel like stopping. However....

"Don't you find that funny, Chuck asking you to drive him? Do you think he's sick?"

"No. He seemed all right. Maybe he just wants to see me...."

"As long as you don't think it's something serious. Say hello to him for me. And tell him to take care of himself. I need a living example before me. Chuck's my proof, he's the one who keeps me hoping. He's been looking tired for a while now."

I had almost guessed right. Chuck was more than just tired, he was not well. He admitted as much to Yves as they drove towards Stanford. He was afraid they were going to keep him at the hospital longer than for a routine check-up. He was having difficulty breathing. According to him his lungs were showing rejection symptoms. Before his transplant in 1981 he had lived all his life as a semi-invalid. His complaint was congenital; he had been born with a malformed ventricle. After he had arrived in California his second chance came so rapidly, and he recovered so quickly, that everything led him to believe he would enjoy a second life for a very long time. He was born in Binghamton, New York, but had adapted to the climate and lifestyle here so well that he had decided to settle in Mountain View permanently. He was working in a funeral home and a liquor store, two jobs that never left him short of jokes. It was with a smile, making a joke of it, that he told Yves he thought he'd arrived at the end of his three years of reprieve. "I'm thirty-three," he said, "and I've come to the end of my public life." That day he was hospitalized.

Through all of May and part of June, Chuck was hooked up to a respirator and left to contemplate the ceiling of the intensive care unit. We went to see him from time to time. Yves would put on his anti-bacteria costume while I had to content myself with watching them gossip from behind the window. They're very careful at Stanford about not spreading infection. As a "recipient" I wasn't allowed to take any risks. All this time Chuck kept on smiling, but the doctors' prognosis was getting more and more sombre. As well as fighting the effects of rejection he was suffering from a kidney infection. He had to be given a very strong dose of medication and to accept the terrible consequence: deafness. "I'll learn to lip-read," he told us.

But even after the doctors' best efforts he didn't improve. Only one solution remained: a second transplant. All the members of the Stanford medical team met to discuss this possibility. It had never been tried before with a heart-lung transplant and the risks were great. The patient was considerably weakened by several weeks of hospitalization; scar tissue left from the first operation would mask guidelines that were indispensable for the surgeons. There was a very small chance the operation would succeed. What were the odds? No one could say. No statistics were available. It would be a world first, and even if the chance of success were only one in a million, it would have to be tried. Because, as I said, Chuck Walker was Stanford's most extraordinary success; he was a symbol and a source of courage not only for us recipients but for anyone who came in contact with him. He had to live!

Even when they had reached this conclusion, the doctors were not out of the woods. For Chuck, as for me and my companions in waiting, the whole dozen of us, the same uncontrollable factor would decide the outcome. Would a compatible donor show up? Time was short. It was a question of weeks or days. And on the morning of June 17 it was possibly a question of hours, when Chuck was prepared for the operating room. As usual, the identity of the donor was kept a closely guarded secret. The operation lasted eight hours, after which Dr. Jamieson, head of the surgical team, declared, "We're in the clear," which meant that his work was done and Chuck's had to begin. His will to live and all the defence mechanisms of his body had to begin their fight.

The day after his second heart-lung transplant Chuck was awake and smiling; three weeks later he was drinking wine with his hospital meals. Thanks to his indomitable will to live, he pulled through. Thanks also to that mysterious accomplice called luck.

But the summer's good surprises weren't over yet. On July 12 it was Monty Baster's turn to get a new heart and lungs. Monty, a strapping young man of nineteen, full of stubborn determination too, announced that he was going to break the record for quick convalescence. And in fact he did recuperate very fast, going through all the stages of his re-education therapy in thirteen days.

But there's another reason why that the little flame of hope—kept alive by so much good news this summer—has suddenly burst into a blaze of joy. Today, July 25, Judy Holden is also going to attempt her rebirth. It's the seventh transplant since my arrival. The second woman. She's been waiting for more than a year. I've put her name down after all those who have had their chance from the very start of cardio-pulmonary transplants at Stanford. In a little notebook I've divided the pages into four columns: number, name, date of operation, date of death. There are only seven X's in the fourth column. That means there are fourteen survivors. And Judy Holden, number 21, is going to be one of them, I'm sure of it. She's another fighter, a daredevil, afraid of nothing, least of all death. And she's a woman! Is it presumptuous of me to hold high hopes for her?

CHAPTER EIGHTEEN

Friendship with a Capital F

September 21, 1984

Since coming to California I've received more than five hundred letters. People of all ages and from all walks of life have written to encourage me—some discreetly or timidly, others without hesitating to share their own misfortunes. Needless to say, I replied at greatest length to the letters that most candidly offered the writer's friendship, particularly when they came at periods when I had some time to devote to them.

Last February I received an envelope from the Federal Correction Centre in Laval. Inside were four handwritten pages that read as follows:

January 28, 1984

Hello Diane!

You don't know us, but we know you well, thanks to the media. We've been following your odyssey for several months now and we must say it certainly doesn't leave us indifferent.

We know that you're living through some very painful times now, and that's why we join you in thought to bring you a little comfort, small as it may be. Your outstanding character, your courage, and your faith in life have inspired us deeply and have shown us the high road to victory through moral fortitude.

It may seem a little strange to receive a letter like this, especially from us, but we too have hearts and love to share with people in distress. So let me introduce us: we are all prisoners serving life sentences. We are also members of what we call the Life Club, which undertakes various humanitarian activities. One of our monthly projects is to try to bring a little joy and love into the lives of people who are suffering one way or another.

Even if we are convicts, we have plenty of friendship and love to share. Who can know better than us the meaning of hope and what it is to be continually straining after freedom? In fact, you and we have a lot in common.

So we will be united with you in thought, hoping for the success of your operation. We earnestly hope a donor will turn up because he will live again in you. And we sincerely hope you will accept our expression of friendship, hope and solidarity, and above all our fraternal love, because we're not a bad lot after all.

We may be far away, but we're very close. Distances don't count; we have you in our thoughts and will be close to you in your trials. Don't be surprised to hear that we pray for you.

Best wishes for a successful operation and may the Lord guide you and grant you all the happiness you so richly deserve.

Prisoners of the Laval Federal Detention Centre.

The fourth page contained the signatures of thirty-six prisoners. I was astonished and moved and very appreciative of the attention shown by this good "bad lot" with such tender hearts, but because of the jumble of moving and various other preoccupations, I didn't get around to thanking them until the end of March. A little later I received a reply letter from Prisoner Number 6083, the young fellow who had been spokesman for the group. In this second letter he described himself briefly: twenty-nine years old, short some teeth, student at Collège Marie-Victorin (by correspondence) working for a diploma in computer science. He is serving a life sentence "with parole eligibility at ten years". He has been incarcerated for five years now and has managed to finish high school, participate in various meetings, and help with secretarial duties. He's a devil for work, resourceful, generous, doesn't count his time, and would give you the shirt off his back. I was completely won over by him. He had included a stamped self-addressed envelope and I replied. That was the beginning of my correspondence with Ghus, and of a Friendship with a capital F.

We have in common a liking for orderliness and clearcut situations and a passion for computers. But perhaps more than all the rest is the fact that we're both living under sentence. That brings us closer together. I feel, as he does, cheated of liberty. Like him, I'm "serving time" with my old lungs and heart, and I don't know if they'll last me long enough to have replacements put in. So I've even less assurance of eventual liberation than he has. He's aware of the injustice of this; he knows he deserves his fate while I did nothing to merit mine. His simplicity and directness touch me. In his letter of July 8, he wrote:

> I've understood so many things since I've been in prison that now I'm a completely different man, in mentality, character, and attitude. Which is why I can express my feelings without embarrassment. You can count on plenty of friendship and love from me because I've got lots to give. I spent too many years repressing my feelings in that damned underworld I lived in. When I say "love", I hope you understand what I mean. It's not my intention to chase after you and if you're afraid of something like that, our relationship will be difficult and I'd prefer to end it now.
>
> You know, when a man begins a friendship with a woman, the question of romance always becomes the principal objective, and yet if men only knew that there is something much more intense, they'd kick themselves. I'm very pleased that you're willing to keep my letters confidential. On the other hand, since Yves is sharing your life, I think he should be let in on them, because he's shown his love and devotion for you. So I haven't any objection to him reading my letters and sharing

our moments of friendship because I think he deserves that. He also deserves my confidence because he's part of you. Anyway, I'll leave all that up to you....

No ambiguity there. No little secrets to hide from my man. He's free to read over my shoulder when I read Ghus's letters, which I always open before all the others. They're often joyful and full of humour, rarely nostalgic, never self-pitying, always positive. Ghus calls himself my "pen pal". Thanks to him I discover the realities of a convict's life, and also benefit from the expert advice of a computer consultant.

But above all Ghus is an energy distributor, and when I feel worn out, as I do tonight—lost, discouraged, fed up with waiting—I think of him. He charges my batteries again. Just imagining him in his little cell playing around with his computer or writing a letter in his big generous handwriting is enough to make me forget my worries.

I find it difficult to explain just why I feel more depressed and vulnerable lately. Nothing alarming has happened. On the contrary, summer has been slipping by very quietly: little fishing trips with Ken and Dorothy, visits to the surrounding countryside with Sylvie, Yves's sister who spent a few days with us—no reason to feel tired or to need my oxygen tank more often. Maybe it's because of autumn coming; I've always found it a sad season. No, I really have no reason to have the blues...even if I won't be with Isabelle on her birthday. After all, I'll soon have her close for a long stretch, because she'll be spending the month of November here with my parents.

So I mustn't let myself get down in the dumps.

I'm supposed to be a model of courage; I've got to keep busy, invent things to do. I'm going to go right away and reply to the letter I got from Ghus this morning, his sixteenth, that began so joyfully: "*Bonjour Tendresse.*" I'll give him my good news, tell him about the upcoming visit, about the courses Yves and I have begun—photography and cooking for Yves, Spanish and computer sciences for me. I'll even write to him on my computer. He'll be proud of his pupil.

As for my gloominess...I won't mention it. That way maybe I'll get around to forgetting it.

CHAPTER NINETEEN

Lullaby for Isabelle

November 29, 1984

I don't want to think about her leaving tomorrow. I want to believe that she'll wake up beside me every day. My pretty little doll is sleeping now, one arm around her pillow, her face turned towards the breaking day. It's an angelic profile: between her forehead and her chubby cheeks her nose just barely projects enough to be seen above the delicate line of her half-opened lips. A portrait by Renoir that I will never tire of contemplating— skin the colour of a peach, hair the colour of wheat, mouth like a smooth tropical shell. I draw you over and over endlessly in my mind, darling daughter, with loving little touches. I imagine your smile just at the point of breaking into laughter. Or I can see you pouting, your hair tousled and stormy. Now, as I lie beside you, I watch a storm cross your face, your nostrils tremble, your pupils move under your eyelids. Seconds later, you're sleeping peacefully. You don't move, your eyes are closed, your hands half-closed. Perhaps it was a dream. You are far away.

I envy you. I turn on to my other side seeking a cool place in the sheets, a hollow in the pillow, that will at last let me fall asleep. Since midnight I've been following the ridiculous trajectory of the hour-hand on the clock. It's 5:22—it will soon be daylight. It's high time I got some sleep because night is on its way out, full of those floating anxieties I breathe in with every breath—the fear of going to sleep for ever, of not waking up with you by my side.... I toss and turn and then get up so I can breathe better.

"Maman? Does your heart hurt?"

"No. Go back to sleep, *ma tourterelle*. I'm just going to get some oxygen and then I'll come and lie down beside you."

"Does it hurt?"

"What, the oxygen? No. It's like a little breeze in your nose."

"It tickles, eh?"

I laugh.

"Yes, that's it. It tickles. Go back to sleep now."

Obediently you close your eyes, confident, ready to find your dreams again. For you life is a mysterious story you discover a little more of every day. You're four now and a fountain of questions. When you ask me if we'll be going back to the big house together, I know you see us both living with your father. You think the only reason I left was to get my heart and lungs changed. You think I'd go back to live with him; you don't know yet that he isn't my husband any more. I told you a long time ago but you were too small, you must have forgotten it. I won't say anything to set you right. What's the use of making you sad or making promises I won't keep? Who knows, for that matter, if I'll be able to go back home? But I want you to think it's still possible.

That's why I didn't tell you that the little girl you were playing with the other day at the hospital has just had heartbreaking news. Her father, who was waiting for a new heart and lungs like me, died a week after the operation. I preferred to hide it from you because that could happen to me too. I didn't really lie to you; I told you part of the truth: the little girl's father did receive what I've been waiting thirteen months for. When you heard that you said, "Next time it's your turn."

"My turn?"

"Yes. The other time it was her daddy's turn, so next time it's my mummy's turn."

I had to smile so you wouldn't see how upset I was. My turn, yes, but for what? To live, or to die? You didn't notice how my voice trembled when I answered, "Yes, maybe it will be my turn."

Afterwards you talked about the big house again. For you it's a memory of happy times, for me a reminder of painful scenes and incessant reproaches. Your child's memory has kept the best parts. That's fine. It's not good for you to know so soon what may lie in store.

Tomorrow when you leave I'll try not to cry. I want you to remember my smile in case you never see it again.

Sleep, my little one, go on thinking that life is as good as a piece of cake with icing on it. Lick your fingers and don't miss a crumb! And while you do, I'm going to soak up your expression so I never forget it: cheeks the colour of apples, forehead like bronze, lips the colour of strawberries....

CHAPTER TWENTY

A Gloomy Prospect

January 8, 1985

Gayle Reedy had his heart-lung transplant on October 27, 1984. A week later he died in the intensive care unit. He was a young farmer from Wisconsin who had brought his family here. His wife and children had been waiting with him for eight months and often came to the meetings; I liked them very much. Like the rest of his family Gayle was modest, simple, sincere, and generous. The heart he left the doctors was a heart of gold. He had two daughters, one of them a little older than Isabelle. He died during my parents' visit.

Andrea Matsushima had the same operation yesterday, seventeen months after she arrived in California. And she had waited fourteen months before being admitted to Stanford. I learned of her death when I telephoned the hospital just now. When she left the operating room the doctors predicted she wouldn't make it. They had tried for twelve hours to give her a second life. Andrea had had serious cardio-pulmonary problems since birth, and at the age of six months she had beaten the survival record of all others afflicted with the same disease. Recently she had been much sicker than I was; at the Christmas meeting I had lent her my oxygen. But she showed such dogged determination to live that I'd never expected such a sudden end.

In my notebook I marked X's opposite their names. Gayle was number 22, Andrea number 23. The surgeons and the medical team feel very bad; they've lost two more patients. Yves and I have lost two friends.

CHAPTER TWENTY-ONE

A Sleepless Night

January 15, 1985

The deaths of Gayle and Andrea can be explained by the fact that both had had other operations before their transplants. That, in brief, is what Dr. Stuart Jamieson confided to me when I saw him in his office at Stanford. The operation to the aorta that I had when I was six may therefore make the surgeons' delicate work more difficult at the time of my graft. Instead of opening the thorax from the trachea to the sternum, they will have to make the opening from front to back, which, according to their calculations, will avoid complications. But for the last two transplants like this they had to clean the thoracic cage before placing the heart and lungs in it, and that caused massive bleeding. The lost blood had to be replaced by transfusions, which resulted in the rejection of the organs.

Dr. Jamieson is candid; he doesn't hide anything from me; besides lowering the success rate, these two setbacks show that my own chances of survival aren't as high as we thought. He told me I had a choice: I could either take the risk with a reduced chance of success and go on waiting for a suitable donor, or I could return home. I didn't hesitate.

"Even if I've got just one chance in a hundred, I'll risk it!"

Now that this first impulsive reaction is over I'm beginning to feel the drag of discouragement.

Besides, winter doesn't help much: my health is deteriorating, and I can feel my strength draining away. I have difficulty getting to sleep at night, and Yves gets worried seeing me toss and turn. I've got a prescription for sleeping pills and tonight after the TV news I took two and slipped him one. That way we'll both have a chance at a good night's sleep.

But it seems to me I heard someone knocking at the door. Was I dreaming? I think I barely dozed off—I must have fallen asleep. What time is it? Just 3:15. Everything seems quiet now. I strain to hear for sure....

"Yves, did you hear that?"

"What?"

"I think there's someone at the door."

"No, you dreamed it. Go back to sleep, Diane."

I'm willing to try but there's the noise again. This time I know I didn't dream it. Three quick knocks.

"Yves, listen!"

"What now?"

"I tell you, someone's knocking."

"Okay, I'll go and see. Wait here."

Wait? Me? No, I get up. I can hear the fire alarm perfectly now. In the living room our new boarder is stretched out on the sofa. It's Cashew, a vigorous young tom-cat we got at the flea market. Yes, I know, it's hardly a place to buy a kitten—he was full of them. But we finally managed to get rid of them. At least I hope so, because the way he's wriggling now.... Yves tells me there's nobody at the door.

"But don't you hear the bell, Yves?"

"Yes, but you know it's always going off for nothing. Come on back to bed, Diane."

"No. I don't like it. I'm going to phone downstairs."

115

No answer at the desk. I look out the window. There's a small group of people on the sidewalk.

"Look down there. What are they doing?"

"Nothing special. They're coming back from a party."

"Seems funny to me."

"Well, not me. Just the same, I'm going to make sure...."

Yves opens the door then closes it immediately.

"Diane! There's smoke! Come on, quick!"

He's already dressed while I'm getting into my leather pants and a sweater. I grab my purse, a coat, and my breathing tube.

"Quick, let's go!"

"Where's Cashew?"

There he is rolled up in a ball on the sofa. I hug him to me. I'm ready. Yves opens the door and takes me up in his arms. The smoke is thick and choking. We're on the third floor but there's no question of taking the elevator. Never mind, the staircase is behind that door on the left. Quick! Oh! A huge cloud of smoke seizes me by the throat. I'm coughing. I pull the sleeve of my coat across my mouth and breathe through it. The walls seem to be on fire but there are no flames, just this dense black smoke. Yves is going down as fast as he can. Cashew lets me hold him close, totally unaware of the danger. Second floor. The smoke burns our eyes. I can't see. How can Yves still go on? At last, only two more doors to go through. Air! Breathe! Pump, heart! Work, lungs!

Outside, the little crowd of people is making signs to us. We must be a pathetic sight: Yves holding me in his arms, me holding the cat to my heart. They tell us we're the last out and we had the bad luck to choose the most dangerous exit, right beside where the fire broke out. What does it matter? We're alive! Throats irritated, noses itchy, but that's all. Nobody's been hurt. The firemen are here and it seems they've got the blaze under control. It started in a bedroom on the second floor.

Well, now we can begin to assess the material damage. Yves and I take refuge in the car and begin to take inventory of our possible losses. I'm particularly concerned about the organ. The rest of the furniture isn't worth much more than the effort it took to find the cheapest stuff possible. Eventually we'd be able to replace all that without much trouble. On the other hand, I'd be much more upset to lose things that were precious to me, like letters, photos, or souvenirs of birthdays or other happy occasions, all those little things that are priceless just because they're irreplaceable. And I hope my plants and fish pulled through all right.... But what's the use of worrying beforehand?

A neighbour in one of the next apartment blocks offers us the hospitality of her kitchen. Warm words and cool drinks calm our nerves; it's great. When we leave about ten o'clock the firemen have gone and the crowd has dispersed. Yves takes me in his arms again and we climb back up to the third floor. It's a desolate sight: doors pulled off their hinges, walls blackened, windows broken, curtains dripping with water and soot. In places ceilings and floors have given way. But when we reach our apartment there's a happy surprise: everything is intact. Nothing has been damaged except the rug—with the firemen's big bootmarks. The plants are turning their leaves towards the light and in the aquarium the fish are still swimming nonchalantly back and forth. On the wall the postcards, photos and holy pictures are all safe, neither wet nor smoky.

"It's a miracle, Yves! You see that picture of Christ that I stuck to the window? The lady who sent it promised that it would protect me and that nothing bad would happen in the room where I stuck it up. She was right. It's a miracle, don't you think?"

My incredulous friend doesn't reply, but he has to admit that our apartment has been saved from fire damage while all the others are in a sorry state. Yves prowls through the two rooms—probably looking for something to prove I was wrong. He doesn't find anything and comes over and sits down beside me.

"So what do you think? Is it a miracle, or not? Admit it once and for all."

"It's quite extraordinary, I admit...."

117

"You see, my Big Pal in the sky doesn't want me in his paradise yet. That gives me more confidence. If he doesn't want me yet, it means I've still got a chance."

Yves says nothing.

"What's the matter, Yves? You find that hard to swallow, eh?"

"No, Diane, I was thinking. This place may still be liveable, but there's an awful smell of smoke. And with all the work that will be going on around here, there'll be dust and paint odours and the air won't be breathable. It'll be very bad for you."

"So?"

"So it seems to me I've got my work cut out for me."

"Work?"

"Yes, finding another apartment, packing all this up and moving again...."

"Moving? Well, why not! That'll give me something else to think about!"

CHAPTER TWENTY-TWO

Our Third Home

February 28, 1985

Our old friends, our very best helpers in time of need, Jimmy and Huguette, offered us their hospitality for the time it took to repair the damaged apartment building. Two weeks later we moved back in. The walls had been washed, the rugs had been cleaned, and the place was liveable again, but the idea of moving had taken hold. Particularly because the owners had decided to make the tenants pay for the renovations, with the result that our rent was going up thirty-five dollars a month.

So we had to start patiently shopping around again and submitting ourselves to the pointed questioning of suspicious landlords: Why weren't we working? Where did our income come from? Would we be able to pay the rent like everyone else? Howard and Diana, a couple of friends of ours, found themselves in a similar situation, wanting a bigger apartment. He had arrived in Stanford a little before me. He too was waiting for a heart-lung transplant and he wanted his son by a first marriage to join them in California. Howard has a pension from his employers in Las Vegas, where he worked as a croupier, and Diana works in a restaurant

at the Hilton. With their modest income they inspired the real
estate agencies with nothing but mistrust. Why go on looking
separately? Why not combine efforts? Better still, why not rent a
house big enough to allow everyone the little bit of privacy they
need?

As for the rest, our requirements were identical: the house
would have to be less than an hour's drive from the hospital. We
duly combed the surroundings of Mountain View and explored
the beautiful Santa Clara Valley as far as San Jose, our farthest
possible limit. This city of about half a million inhabitants is
situated in a region of great natural beauty surrounded by green
hills dotted with vineyards and orchards. A peaceful décor, all in
soft shades of colour.

"I like this country, Yves. We'll be happy here."

Yves parked the car on the asphalt drive of a huge house built
on the side of a hill.

"Whoa, Diane! That looks like a castle to me. The ad didn't
mention any price, did it? Now I know why. It's certainly way
too much for us."

"Well, you never know," I said, though I was somewhat put
off by the luxury of the place too.

Yves got out of the Honda, walked around the property and
then came back and sat down beside me with a woebegone look.

"It's not for us, Diane. Swimming pool, fireplace—no sense
dreaming in technicolour, it's a rich people's home."

"Do you think so?"

Howard and Diana shared his opinion: no sense setting our
sights on this inaccessible castle. All the way back I daydreamed,
watching the green hills out the window. It would be so relaxing
to have that view every day. As soon as we got back to the
apartment, I called the number in the ad. I had to wait for the
agent to go through her lively, detailed description of the place
(four bedrooms, two bathrooms, kitchen and dining room, living
room with open fireplace), which just whetted my appetite.

"Yes, but how much?"

She went on praising the superb countryside and the other advantages we had already had occasion to appreciate for ourselves before cautiously proposing: "$1,250 a month."

Was I hearing right? I immediately divided the sum in two. $625 for each couple? It was a bargain! I insisted we meet her as soon as possible. Provided with irrefutable proof of our seriousness as clients—letters from the Optimist Club and the doctors at Stanford—Yves and I had soon won the young woman over with the charm of our inimitable accent and the story of our adventures. Full of sympathy and understanding, and acutely aware of the circumstances that threatened Howard's life and mine, she offered to put us at the top of the waiting list, for the final decision wasn't hers to make. A few days later we visited the inside of our future home—that's right, we are the new tenants, and it's even bigger and better than we imagined!

Yves is more than pleased with the pretty, practical kitchen and its wide ceramic counters. The aquarium will fit perfectly in the dining room. I have my eye on the biggest of the four bedrooms; I've decided it will suit us fine. Diana and Howard agree to take the one at the back and the one next to that can be for Howard's son. That leaves one over for guests. What fun to invite Isabelle to such a big house!

Now we'll have to see about filling all these huge rooms. Like us, our friends have only the modest furnishings of a young couple, but Howard has a few other things in his home town. Yves and Diana went with him to Las Vegas to collect this furniture and his fifteen-year-old son. Yves told me the adventures of this happy troupe when he got back. The old pickup they had borrowed from a friend caused them more worries than trouble and they returned laden like thieves, for Howard's "few things" turned out to be much more than expected.

Meanwhile I made plans and organized our future home on paper so all we had to do was pack up and transport our belongings to San Jose. For once Yves got out of this chore, because the insurance company paid for the packing and moving.

121

Here we are at last, almost settled in. Without fussing about the disorder everywhere I look out the window at a landscape turning to gold under the setting sun. Cows and horses graze on the new grass in the fields. The mountains in the distance are tipped with pink clouds. The scene is set for the third act of our California adventure, and I prefer not to think of the verdict of my cardiologist—who predicted that by now I would have only two months left to live.

CHAPTER TWENTY-THREE

A Taste for Life

April 18, 1985

You never get used to seeing your friends die. It's always a cruel blow you blame on fate, not being able to pin the blame elsewhere. But the danger that threatens the life of us recipients is too real for us to despair or give in when faced with this injustice. The death of others mustn't weaken us. It's a question of survival; if we don't hold our heads high under the attack, we risk becoming the next victims ourselves. We must be in a state of readiness for war. We're here at Stanford as though on a strange battlefield. Our common enemy is Death. We must all fight his attacks, without becoming preoccupied with lives cut down beside us.

This combative attitude is not always easy to sustain, and is often replaced by one of resignation. That's what happened three weeks ago when I learned of John Tedeschi's death. John had received a heart-lung transplant in the early spring. He was a Bostonian, born of Italian parents, and had worked for several years as a draftsman in an advertising agency. He had Eisenmenger's disease, a congenital illness whose symptoms only develop slowly. He had come to Stanford alone, which was probably why Yves and I got to be friends with him so soon. From the very first meeting, despite our linguistic isolation, we were drawn to this solitary man who loved life just the same. He was one of the first to bring a bottle of wine to our hospital reunions, which helped liven up the atmosphere. "Life's too short not to enjoy it," he used to say.

Later we often visited him during his convalescence. He was getting along well but didn't pay much attention to his doctors' orders; he disagreed with hospital routine, neglected the breathing exercises that were recommended, and wilfully forgot to take his medication. In short, he went on acting in the nonchalant way we'd always associated with him. But as useful as this indifferent attitude was before the operation, afterwards it turned against him. He was playing with his life, flirting with death. Once released from the hospital, he went on leading a disorderly life and was obliged to return for hospitalization for longer and longer periods.

That's why I was scarcely surprised to hear of his death. John had refused to accept the indispensable fight for survival. In a certain way he had chosen to die, had dug his own grave. This interpretation may seem cruel and disrespectful to his memory, but I think he would have agreed with it. I am impelled to find reasons to explain this kind of setback, which they prefer to call by a different name in hospital circles. And quite rightly so. A doctor is never the only one to earn the success of a cure. Most frequently he is ready to grant his patient most of the merit, attributing it to his or her will to live. So it seems logical to me not to blame science for certain failures, but here, too, to give patients their due.

Stories like John's act on me like a cold shower. They make me want to shake myself and be up and doing. Or is it the tonic effect of this springtime, which is even more noticeable because of the particularly abundant vegetation? It seems to me this season has always been good to me. I feel a new surge of energy and want to start working again.

I didn't have to look far for a way to use my spare time. In the mailbox, which is always full of junk mail, I recognized a familiar catalogue. I had sold Avon products before I was married and had found it an amusing experience. All you had to do was show the products, fill out the order forms, and send them to the company, then take around the client's soap or perfume. It was easy as pie, and Yves would certainly help me.

"What do you say to earning a little extra cash, Yves?"

"Hmm?"

"A little pocket money wouldn't go amiss, would it?"

He agreed to help as soon as I said I'd split the profits with him. Which was fair because he'd be doing half the work—that is, he'd walk along beside my wheelchair, and if necessary carry me up to the front porch of the houses we visited. I'd do all the rest until we delivered the products, which we would do together the same way.

To begin with we chose a long, straight street with lots of houses. We were an instant success. People were surprised or moved by my unusual means of transportation. That was how I got to know a lot of people in the neighbourhood. Everything went very smoothly until it came time to share the profits.

"Hey! What's this? Only two-fifty?" he complained, when I gave him his part.

"Listen, Yves, I've run out of bath oil and body lotion and I took advantage of the opportunity to replenish my make-up kit. It's much less expensive this way. You've no idea how much I saved over the drugstore prices. Next time your part will be bigger, you'll see."

Okay. That's the way it is. You can see he's not too keen on my new job. On the other hand he's much more interested in my participation in *The Gift of Life*. I already spoke about it; it's that little newsletter put out by and for the Stanford recipients. To begin with I worked on the cover and changed the layout and the graphics. But two weeks ago I was named editor-in-chief. Now I write a short editorial, try to collect information that will be useful to my colleagues, and take care of the layout of the whole thing. Right now I'm working on the June–July issue, which promises to be a mine of interesting information. I've already collected newspaper stories, among them an interview with Mary Gohlke, the first person to receive a new heart and lungs at Stanford. There will also be a lead article by a certain Dr. Cooper from Toronto, an interview by my colleague Marsha with a Stanford doctor, and a great many stories about transplants and organ donations. All told, fifty or so photocopied pages, stapled together and sent to a hundred subscribers.

This issue also carried an article on Chuck Walker that had appeared in the *Times Tribune*. I've told about the circumstances of Chuck's deafness last spring. Until Yves and I had much improved our English, Chuck was incapable of appreciating our progress. Although he had learned to lip-read, he couldn't grasp our words, because of our way of speaking. We had to settle for shorter and more and more silent visits. But our first problem was to alert him to our presence, since he couldn't hear the doorbell. One day Yves had to try all sorts of crazy things; he climbed on to the balcony and, seeing that the doors were open a crack but locked in that position, tried to attract Chuck's attention by tossing things into the room. Chuck sat there, his eyes glued to the TV. Yves had practically emptied his pockets before he finally hit the target with a coin. Chuck shrugs off these difficulties, though they don't always have happy endings.

From now on, however, that type of incident will be avoided thanks to a new companion who will serve as Chuck's ears. It's a little dog specially trained to react to different bells: the doorbell, the telephone, the alarm clock, or the oven-timer. Forty such hearing-ear dogs are lent out in California every year, says the Palo Alto *Times Tribune*, and Chuck is delighted with his, a black terrier pup who is very sweet. The only inconvenience is that now he's lost his excuse for sleeping in in the morning.

This is the kind of little news item I like to run in *The Gift of Life*. It means I have to sort through the information provided by our subscribers or people interested in the publication. It's fascinating work which requires a certain method and sense of organization, and satisfies my insatiable curiosity. I also love poring over magazines looking for the little joke or caricature that will lighten up contents that otherwise might be too heavy.

As for the editorial, Yves likes to help me find the ideas and we write it up together. Our English has improved considerably, and my assistant, Marsha, insists on publishing our text the way it stands, even if it contains a few blunders. Yves has had some excellent ideas for improving the appearance of the bulletin. He's the one who thought of setting up the titles of our articles on the front page the way they do in the newspapers. My man is proud of his initiatives and is rediscovering the pleasure of working. He looks after the photocopying and distribution too.

I admit that this second job brings me more satisfaction than the first. But I refuse to spend days on end locked up in our big bedroom, which is the editor-in-chief's main office. When the weather is fine I go out and distribute my Avon catalogues. Jason, Howard's son, comes with us sometimes. And despite all these activities I still find time to stretch out by the swimming pool and think, like Mary Gohlke, "Life is precious and magnificent. And until someone who has passed over comes back down to tell me, 'Hey! It's fantastic up there!' I'm hanging on to this earth for dear life, as long as I live."

CHAPTER TWENTY-FOUR

Emergency

June 25, 1985

"Yves, something's wrong. I'm hurting all over. Do you think it's that cyst again?"

"I don't know, Diane.... Where exactly?"

"Here, in my chest. I can't breathe. I'm suffocating! Oh, Yves. I think I'm going to call the doctor."

"No!"

Yves didn't waste any time. He dialed 911, the emergency number. Chest pains certainly weren't symptoms of the illness that had so frightened me in Montreal in 1983. My cyst had also given me cause for concern twice in California but this was different: the pain filled the whole region of my thorax. An unbearable pain, and much more worrisome because of its location. Yves paced back and forth in front of the window waiting for the ambulance while I tried to calm down. At last I heard a siren...the firetruck....

"Is there a fire someplace?"

"No, they're stopping here."

Yves is jittery and getting mad.

"Bunch of idiots! I told them to send an ambulance. Hurry up, can't you!"

But the over-zealous firemen weren't ready to take off yet. They insisted on asking the "patient" a series of questions: "Where does it hurt?" "How long have you had this pain?" And so on and so forth...while I writhed in agony.

"Yves, answer for me.... The pain's too much.... I can't...."

Yves was becoming more and more impatient. He shouted, "Can't you see she can't answer!"

No, they couldn't, and they left without hurrying. At last the ambulance arrived. A second interrogation. Yves lost his temper.

"Leave her alone and let's get out of here! Quick, to the Stanford Hospital!"

The driver looked over at the medic as though Yves had blurted out an obscenity.

"Sorry, mister," he said, "I only take people to the San Jose Hospital."

"What the hell!" Yves had to insist, to explain that I was under the care of the Stanford doctors, that I was waiting for a transplant, and all the rest. The driver was adamant; what he did was take patients to the hospital at San Jose. Yves had to resort to threats and anger. He blew his top:

"You're totally incompetent! Get out! I'll take her myself. Can't you see she's *dying*!"

Maybe he was exaggerating, but that's exactly how I felt—as though my heart had started to swell and was going to burst at any minute. The medic took a quick look at me, nodded to the driver, and at last they took me down to the ambulance. But as if they were doing it on purpose, they took the longest way there, the scenic route, and got stuck in a traffic jam.

"Put on your flashers and get the siren going, for God's sake!" Yves shouted.

"That'll be a hundred dollars extra," the phlegmatic ambulance driver replied.

Yves looked at me uncertainly. "How's it going?"

"No better, no worse...," I said, trying to smile.

"Okay. Forget the flashers, but get a move on!" my impatient companion growled.

As for me, I was thinking of the two deaths that had occurred in June, a few days apart: Barry Davis's, which had been quite foreseeable, and Mike McClennan's, which was more of a surprise. Was I going to die too, and, unlike them, without even having my "second chance"? As if I had been speaking aloud, the driver suddenly seemed to understand that we were in a hurry to get there and stepped on the gas. I watched the yellow foliage of the palm trees along the boulevard rushing by and then saw the fountains in front of the hospital. Luckily we didn't have to wait more than a few minutes before Dr. Morris arrived.

After a rapid examination he immediately reassured me—it wasn't what I was afraid of. Once again my cyst had had little ones and had caused an inflammation outside the infected area. My enfeebled state of health had made me suspect cardio-pulmonary complications. No, there was no reason to worry about that. Just like the other three times, there was nothing to do but wait for the cyst to reabsorb itself. Rest, relaxation, a day or two in hospital, and then I could go home again.

This diagnosis should have reassured me—my heart must be very strong to resist such pain. But in fact, to have to fight and struggle exhausts me unnecessarily and makes me use up what little strength I have left. Tonight, taking my make-up off in my hospital room, I spent some time studying my face. The light tan couldn't hide the flabby, dull texture of my skin and my lips.

"Look, Yves, my lips are all blue."

"Not more than usual...."

"Yes they are, they're worse, just look!"

Yves lowers his eyes. I know he's more and more worried about me. He touches me at night when I've finally stopped moving and have dropped off to sleep. He's checking to see if I'm still breathing. He's afraid....

"Yves, I think I'm dying. I want to go back home."

"No, Diane. Dr. Morris said tomorrow. You can sleep at home tomorrow."

"You don't understand anything, Yves. I'm talking about Montreal. I'm fed up with California, fed up with waiting for a donor who never shows up."

"Listen, Diane, you say that because you're worn out. It's a reaction to all that heavy pain. You need rest. I'm going to let you sleep and tomorrow I'll come and get you. We won't need an ambulance this time, will we?"

He's managed to make me laugh. It's true, Yves is right, I am very tired. After a good night's sleep I'll feel better. I'm going to get my strength back and be beautiful again. Yves tickles my lips with his moustache wishing me a good night. I snuggle my head into the pillow, close my eyes, and answer, "Till tomorrow. You'll see, I'll be in great shape."

But for the first time since I've been in California I doubt it. For the first time I don't believe it any more....

CHAPTER TWENTY-FIVE

A Sign from Heaven

August 16, 1985

I can't believe it. I can see a path ahead of me. Until this morning
the sky was covered, the horizon invisible, the fog so dense I
didn't know where to put my foot down to move ahead.

For some time now the atmosphere in our big house has
been becoming more and more insufferable. A state of war
exists between Diana and me. The looks we exchange are worse
than words; they're whiplashes that keep the quarrel going. The
presence of our respective mates, far from improving the stormy
climate, makes it worse; their easy companionship makes us
guiltier. They seem to be watching us as if we were animals in
a zoo and that makes us furious. Yves is no help: he just talks
about sitting on the fence—a picket fence—and Howard adds,
"My father was right; he always used to say, 'A woman in the
house is one too many.' I think we've overdone it."

I don't know which of us is more to blame. I realize she has
the more thankless role because she has to work outside the
home. Howard looks after the house for her, and what she can't
accept is that I don't participate like him and Yves in the hundred

and one little things that have to be done to meet her standards. She thinks I'm selfish or lazy, and I find myself playing into her hands by locking myself up in my room. It's the only way I can avoid her squalling voice which I could never match in violence. Whenever I try to turn up my own volume it brings on breathlessness and coughing fits. That's why I slam the door and take refuge in my bed.

Prolonged periods confined to our lovely big room are slowly undermining my morale. The telephone is silent most of the day, and the mail has diminished considerably. My Quebec friends are becoming as tired as I am of waiting for the improbable donor. Especially since one paper ran the headline "Diane's doctors are giving up on her." It wasn't and isn't true! It's not the doctors who are giving up, it's life that's leaving me—life like a faintness in the breath, leaving nothing but a murmur for a voice.

"Yves, Yves, I can't go on. I want to get out of here.... I want to go home."

"Diane, we've talked about this every day now for a month. There's no question of going back to Montreal. You know very well there's no chance for you there."

"Or here either, Yves. Less and less. The donors are too big. I've lost confidence."

"Well, I haven't, if you want to know, and we're not leaving here unless we have very good reasons to go somewhere else. If you're so set on moving, find a city where they do transplants. In Arizona, in France, in England if you like, but not in Quebec. There's no sense arguing, Diane. I won't go home with you. I refuse to sign your death warrant."

Every time we have this discussion Yves gets more inflexible. He always has the last word, and that doesn't leave anything to do but start all over again. One evening, after going through the same old song and dance, I was more discouraged than ever. I seemed to have hit bottom; it was impossible to sink lower.

So, instinctively, I raised my head to the heavens and called on my Big Pal in the sky. At least he wouldn't talk back. On this occasion, however, that's exactly what I wanted; this time I prayed he would reply. Up until then I hadn't been very demanding. I'd prayed every day without asking for anything, without bugging him too much, just to let him know that if he felt like calling someone to be with him, he might as well choose a person about my size who had signed an organ-donor card and lived, if possible, within a sixty-mile radius of San Jose.... Of course, I wasn't twisting his arm; if that wasn't the way he saw things, his will be done. But this time, I admit, I put the pressure on a little, because I was at the end of my tether. I told him, "Listen, God, your silence is a wondrous thing, but give me the means of interpreting it. The way it is, I don't understand a thing; I don't know what's going on. I can't see the path you've prepared for me any more. Am I supposed to stay here or leave? Answer me, please! If you don't want to speak to me, I'll understand; I'm probably not enough of a saint to hear your voice. But just give me a sign, any old sign, and you'll see how quick I'll be to interpret it." Then I went to bed and fell into a deep, dreamless sleep.

The answer wasn't long in coming. This morning I received a letter with two clippings in it for the news section of our bulletin *The Gift of Life*. Eve Savory, a journalist with CBC in Toronto, thought the information might be useful. Indeed, one of the items has completely lifted my spirits. It's a short report of a successful heart-lung transplant performed in Toronto by a Dr. Cooper—we published an interview with him in our newsletter, but I didn't know he performed this kind of transplant.

TORONTO (CP) A 28-year-old mother from Newfoundland has received two new lungs and a heart at Toronto General Hospital, the second such transplant operation here.

A team led by chest surgeon Joel Cooper performed the six-hour operation Thursday. The patient who has not been identified, was in critical but stable condition Friday.

Dr. Tom Todd, a surgeon on the team, said the outlook for the patient is optimistic. While she was suffering primary pulmonary hypertension, a usually fatal disease, she has not had the damage to the other organ and body systems often seen in older patients.

She was awake and alert Friday, although her breathing was being assisted by a ventilator.

The team performed its first double lung and heart operation a year ago on a 60-year-old New York man, Morton Levine, who died of complications a month later.

DIED IN ACCIDENT

The donor of the lungs and heart transplanted Thursday was a 17-year-old man who was fatally injured in a traffic accident four days ago. The donor's eyes and kidneys were also used for transplants.

In the operation, the woman's heart was removed first, then her lungs, and a heart-lung machine replaced the organs until the transplanted ones were ready to take over. A connection was made to the patient's windpipe and then to the aorta, the major blood vessel, and to the right upper chamber of the heart.

Several heart-lung operations have been performed at University Hospital in London, Ont., on patients with heart disease that had affected their lungs.

But Toronto General is the only centre that performs heart-lung transplants on patients with lung conditions.

The first double transplant in London was done on John Adams of Thunder Bay, Ont., who marked his second anniversary May 23.

About 20 such transplants have been done at Stanford Medical Centre in California, but they were also performed on patients with heart disease, rather than with primary lung disease.

I could hardly have hoped for a clearer and more convincing sign. I told Yves the incredible news and he was able to get an appointment with Dr. Jamieson this afternoon. It turns out he knows his Toronto colleague and his work well and is quite ready to let me leave Stanford. He sees no major obstacle in transferring the dossier if Dr. Cooper agrees to put me on his waiting list. He did tell Yves, however, that Joel Cooper is a modest man who doesn't like the publicity that accompanies certain medical situations. Besides, he's very demanding with his patients.

"Demanding? What's that supposed to mean, Yves? That he makes them run before he'll operate on them?"

I feel like laughing tonight. Yves, on the other hand, has that reflective look he saves for times of change.

"Don't be so sure of yourself, Diane. From what I hear, Dr. Cooper chooses his patients as meticulously as he does his medical team. I have the impression that your lifestyle is going to change inside out."

"Bah! We'll see about that. Anyway it's not really important. For me, the only thing that counts is getting closer to Montreal. And Toronto's right next door. Oh, Yves! I'm already thinking of the family Christmas we could have...."

"You're always thinking about partying and having fun!"

"It's true. It's my way of staying alive. It's a way of holding on to hope. But what about you? What are you thinking about that's so awfully profound, eh? No, no, don't say anything. I think I can guess the depth and gravity of your problem. You're already thinking about the move, aren't you? About all those miles you'll have to cover in the little Honda crammed to the gills?"

"No, you're wrong. I was wondering how someone could be so mulish and so birdbrained at the same time."

"You've got your nerve! If you don't skip the zoological observations, I'll leave you behind in California."

"You're so sure you'll be accepted in Toronto?"

"Yes, Yves, absolutely certain. Something tells me that this time we're on the right track."

"And what's your proof?"

"Proof? You'd make fun of me. I'd rather not say just yet. No, I'm not going to tell you."

Because what would Yves think of a mulish, birdbrained female who has a faith to move mountains?

CHAPTER TWENTY-SIX

Equal to Equal

September 16–27, 1985

"What? Refused? Who made that decision? I want to speak to Dr. Cooper immediately...."

Naturally, the doctor isn't in his office. I have to leave a message and call back several times before reaching him. Even then, he's pretty skimpy with explanations at his end of the line. In fact, he lets me do the talking, so I tell him how even twenty-two months of waiting haven't discouraged me. Does he want to put me to the test, to see how strong my determination is? Well, if he wants to see evidence of my insistence, I'll insist. Yet even this moving speech doesn't seem to convince him. He won't give me the answer I want. He won't say, "You're admitted!" All he says, in a very calm voice, is, "You can come and take some tests in Toronto. Choose the dates that suit you best and tell my secretary. And another thing—I don't want to see a single journalist in the hospital. Do you understand?"

"Uh...yes.... Okay, I'll be seeing you."

Yves pokes his nose around from behind his newspaper:

"Is it yes or no?"

"Neither one nor the other. It's going to depend on the tests...."

"What's eating you? You seem disappointed. Are you afraid you'll be turned down? It's more difficult than you thought, isn't it?"

"No, I'm sure to be admitted. What I'm not so sure about is how I'm going to get along with that kind of a doctor."

"I warned you, Diane, and do you know what? I'm glad for you. I've always thought you should have a doctor who could stand up to your caprices, someone who could shout you down."

"He's not a shouter, but he seems to know what he wants."

"That's just what I was saying, someone as stubborn as you."

"Hmm.... And now what am I going to do about all those journalists who want to know what my plans are?"

"Tell them the truth, that your doctor has forbidden you to see them."

"You think it's going to be easy to turn them away? After all, it's thanks to their papers and TV programs that I've been able to manage up till now. I owe them my popularity and the generosity of the public."

"And they owe you increased circulation and ratings. They don't have to follow your every footstep to keep their public informed. They'll be happy with what you tell them. Anyway, we've got other things to think about right now."

That's right: advise Howard and Diana of our departure, collect our few things together, say goodbye to our friends. Yves feels unhappy about leaving our adoptive country; he'll have time, during the three weeks I'll be hospitalized in Toronto, to say goodbye less hurriedly and distribute our excess baggage among our friends.

Last excursion to Santa Cruz, last meeting, last dinner parties with Jimmy and Huguette and Ken and Dorothy, last expedition with Chuck—none of these farewells shakes my morale. The prospect of being nearer my family dispels any hint of nostalgia. I've dreamed of this trip back home too often not to savour every last aspect of it. Time flies as if I were beginning to move once more after a long halt, as if I were coming out of an interminable night. What a wonderful sensation to be moving again! I like it when everything goes very fast! I like speed because it prevents me from turning my head and lingering over people and things. I need to pick out a point up ahead and rush madly towards it. It's an escape, yes, an escape that has kept me alive. I don't want to look back, I want to look ahead where everything is new. "See you soon, Yves! Say goodbye to California for me. Tell it I like it fine and I'm leaving behind some of my best memories: I'll come back and collect them another day."

I've left before the plane does, a premature take-off, but I don't feel any useless grief. What purpose would be served by mulling over my regrets or listing the pros and cons of those twenty-three months? They're gone, finished, vanished behind the clouds. Who's to say that the wait was in vain? I'm the only one who knows how much energy I expended in the waiting. I refuse to look at my bluish fingers or my wasted body; what I lost in physical well-being, I gained in confidence. I hear my heart beating in my chest, the plane leaves the ground, I feel wonderful. I'm glad to be here, happy at the attention lavished on me again. I'm the centre of attention, people talk to me. I'm alive and well.

When I get to Toronto an ambulance is to take me to the hospital. That way Dr. Cooper hopes to avoid any "unfortunate encounters". At all events, I haven't told anyone the date or time of my arrival. Who was it then that tipped off the little group of journalists who are apparently waiting for me in the airport? In order to avoid them the ambulance comes right out on the tarmac and I'm taken off through the tail exit of the plane.

"And my bags? Who'll get my bags?"

"We can't wait," the driver tells me. "We'll get them later."

It's raining. Stretched out here in the dark I listen to the gentle swish of wet tires on the asphalt. It's true, it's autumn; I can't wait to see what it looks like. I can see the lights of skyscrapers on a background of night sky; we're headed downtown. But the journalists have intercepted us; we're being followed. Despite the driver's evasive tactics, the ambulance has been spotted and we make our entry chased through the streets of Toronto. In a last attempt to shake our pursuers, the driver chooses a side entrance instead of Emergency, but to no avail; the reporters and photographers are already there, notebooks and cameras at the ready.

It's really pouring now, but my stretcher gets no shelter from the rain or from the flashbulbs. The medics try to rush me past. "No questions!" they say. Me, I'm laughing, and soaked through. "These will be great pictures for your papers," I tease. I can't help talking to them; I'm so glad to see them. They are glad to see me too, I think. But there's no time to elaborate: I'm pushed along, and the door closes.

Compared to Stanford the Toronto General is a big factory. Several large buildings connected by tunnels. Miles of corridors, an elevator to the tenth floor, then the quiet and comfort of my room.

And what about my bags? Here I am in Toronto with nothing but my purse and a few toilet articles. I want my bags! Alas they won't show up until next day, after I've had plenty of time to show off my impatience and bad humour to all the hospital staff. A great way to get acquainted! This way there will be no surprises; everyone will know what to expect. But my moods are as changeable and my outbursts as short as a summer storm. The nurses are kind and manage to turn my troubles into laughter.

Two days later when Dr. Cooper's visit is announced, I've got back my smile and my baggage.

I refuse to wear the ridiculous hospital gown and I've taken some trouble with my make-up. Perhaps that's why when he sees me he says, "You don't look sick!"

"That's just appearances. I don't like looking sick. You must have read my dossier; I weigh eighty-three pounds."

"Just so. What are you waiting for? Why don't you eat that up?"

I don't like the tone or the look he casts at my untouched tray. I hate spinach quiche.

"I'm not hungry."

He stares down at me as though I were a little girl.

"You have to eat. My patients have to be healthy."

I really wonder what prompts me to retort, "The food's better on the plane than in the hospital. I was treated like a queen, you know."

Now I've really put my foot in it!

"I know," he's quick to reply. "You made a very impressive entry into Toronto. The journalists were even telephoning here. But I warned you—I don't want a star for a patient."

I don't answer. I look him straight in the eye but he looks right back. No, decidedly, I don't like this doctor. What does he think he is, a dictator or something?

"Listen carefully," he goes on, very self-assured. "You're going to follow our rules and obey our instructions. You need to build up your strength again and that's what you're here for. Don't forget it."

Then he looks over the chart where my temperature, blood pressure, and the results of various tests are recorded. He's increasing my oxygen dose and telling me to take it continuously. He's lost his authoritarian air and seems anxious to be well understood, as if the state of my health is of prime importance to him. He jots down some more notes in his little book and then takes his leave, very politely, without familiarity, a little as though he were saying goodbye to another man.

CHAPTER TWENTY-SEVEN

Guinea Pig

September 28–October 15, 1985

My stay in this hospital isn't any bed of roses. Every day I'm put through tests I already know off by heart: blowing into tubes, having my heart and lungs photographed in every nook and cranny, echographs, X-rays, electrocardiograms, the whole business—topped off with daily tests of blood pressure, blood, and urine. Other tests are new, like the one where I have to walk on a treadmill with an apparatus strapped to my ear to measure the concentration of oxygen in my blood. All my bodily functions are under observation; my least reactions are noted; I've become a machine, a file card, a guinea pig.

Yes, a guinea pig. When I was in California a woman wrote accusing me of being just that. It was a surprising letter, the only negative one in the 711 I received. It ran something like this: "You are too intelligent to let yourself be used as an experimental subject.... You mustn't believe everything the doctors tell you.... In your place I would think much more carefully about what was going on...." I doubt that she really wanted to get me down; she mainly wanted to share her skepticism about medicine with me.

Her way of thinking is certainly not unique; there must be plenty of people who mistrust the medical establishment. But not me. Probably at the root of my unshakeable faith in medicine is the operation to my aorta I had when I was six that was a complete success and allowed me to live a normal life. This surgery had no bad after-effects and was in no way related to the subsequent deterioration of my health. That's why I look on a transplant as a second chance to prolong my life. I put my body into the hands of the hospital staff with good grace and the assurance that they know its workings better than I do. I think of myself as being in a huge garage here, in a vast repair shop where I can trust the expert mechanics.

That being said, I don't abandon myself blindly to their slightest demands. I let them know it when the parade of nurses marches in and out too quickly. Hey! Give me time to breathe, can't you? I'm human after all! Why don't you let me sleep in the morning? Is it absolutely necessary to weigh me at seven a.m. and stick a thermometer in my mouth and a needle in my arm at the same time? The answer is simple: certain nurses finish their shifts at eight and are in a hurry to get their day over with. Then it's breakfast and the visits begin, one to mop out the room, another to empty the wastebasket, yet another to change my towels or take my tray. The hospital employs a huge staff, without even counting its doctors, nurses, and interns, who also pop in and out all morning long until lunchtime. After that I close the door, hang out my *Do not disturb* sign, and settle back for a blissful hour of my favourite TV soap opera, *The Young and the Restless*. It's religiously following this American program that helped me improve my English in California. In Toronto I'm really spoiled: every day I get a new episode and a repeat of yesterday's. I'm not the only one addicted to the series; Elma, a nurse's aide, has followed it since the start and has given me a detailed account of the very first adventures. So I'm not entirely cut off from my adoptive country. And of course everyone here speaks the language I've had time to pick up. Nevertheless I'm surprised that in a hospital this big and this close to Montreal there isn't anyone around to chat with in French.

I set out to see if I can find someone, prowling around the corridors, for I'm not allowed to leave the floor, let alone the hospital. At the nurses' station they tell me there is indeed a patient "with a French name", so I head straight for the room of a Monsieur St-Amant. He comes from New Brunswick and is here taking tests to see if he needs a heart-lung transplant. His condition seems less acute than mine, though, and he will soon be going home again. It's good to talk French, like finding a friend in a crowd of strangers. And it's while visiting him that I meet Pierrette Côté, who works for the French Medical Welcoming Service and acts as a liaison with the Toronto Francophone community. It will be thanks to her that my network of contacts expands, and through her that I meet my dearest friends, who will participate most closely in the continuation of my adventure.

As time goes by, too quickly or too slowly depending on the rhythm of my tests, I adapt to my new life. I put up with certain more painful tests—"blood gas", for instance, taken in the artery in the wrist—with exemplary patience. Yes, it hurts, I admit it without complaining, let's get it over with quickly and say no more about it. As in those first days of waiting in California, I fervently nurse the hope that my turn on the operating table will come soon. Unlike Stanford, since the transplant program is very recent there are not a lot of potential recipients. But I have met a young woman from Chicago, Mary Grudzein, who is also waiting for a compatible donor, and we encourage each other. The fact that the waiting list is so short seems promising, and I think my chances are better here. I've met Terry Buckten, Toronto's number three. He got a new heart and lungs on the first of September and he's very well.

I have the impression that in the three weeks I've been here I've gained strength. It's true I've been on oxygen again, and I've been doing my best to eat well. When Yves finally appears at the door of my room this afternoon, the 15th of October, he looks more tired than I do. But the trip went well. This time he had a passenger, not very talkative but good company just the same.

"Where is he now?"

"I left him in the car."

"All alone?"

"He's got food and water and his sleeping bag and he won't be too hot or too cold because I parked in the shade. He'll be able to look out the window. Don't worry, he's got his basket."

It's lucky Cashew doesn't get bored easily because he's going to have to spend two more days in the car. Cats aren't allowed in the nurses' residence where they can put up a few visitors to Toronto General. Yves will be staying there a couple of nights. I'm so glad to see my man again; I've got a thousand things to tell him. First about my new friends and how I managed to get along without him these past three weeks, then about my great decision. It's a plan that's kept me tingling for the past five days.

"Dr. Cooper will never agree to that, Diane. You'd better forget about it."

"He hasn't the right to refuse me that pleasure. I don't give a damn about his permission...."

"Has he at least put you on the waiting list?"

"No, that's just it. I won't know before October 24. You see, the whole team have to give their consent. Oh Yves! I can't tell you how I've been dreaming of it. It's been almost two years now...."

"Okay. Let's wait to see Dr. Cooper."

By chance Dr. Cooper drops by shortly after. In Yves's presence he takes his authoritarian tone again; he wants an ally, an accomplice. He repeats, as he does at every visit, that I should gain some weight.

"You must sleep and eat well and build up your strength. Don't think of anything else but getting healthy. You want to put every chance you can on your side. Take oxygen twenty-four hours a day."

"Even at night?"

"All the time!"

Yves seems to be impressed by this seemingly cold character. He doesn't say a word. It's a bad time to talk to the doctor about my plan. Too bad, I charge in anyway and blurt it out. The doctor's face remains impassive; he doesn't answer. I insist:

"You can't refuse me. It would be inhuman. It's two years since I've seen my city. Five months since I held my little girl in my arms."

"How long would you be away?"

"A week, just seven days. I'll be back on October 24, the day I'll at last get on your waiting list. Since I'm not officially admitted yet, what difference can it make to you?"

For a few moments he hesitates, looking embarrassed.

"If a donor turns up during that week it will be your own responsibility."

"Yes, I know. I've thought of that. I'll take the risk; it'll be my fault."

"Very well, then. I suppose I can't refuse you this little trip. But I warn you, you're not to tell any journalists about your departure."

Yves looks across at me. Does he doubt my good intentions?

"I promise, Dr. Cooper."

Before leaving he glances at Yves again, just to make sure he has his support. Yves nods. Ah, that silent male complicity! Just the same....

"I got him, didn't I?"

"Yes, but I think he knows you pretty well, Diane. You'd have done what you wanted anyway, isn't that so?"

"It's true. I wanted it so much it was overpowering, irresistible. I need a week's holiday."

"You deserve it. Let's just hope that you...that you won't live to regret it...."

CHAPTER TWENTY-EIGHT

Homecoming

October 17–24, 1985

It's incredible—nothing has changed. I'm coming back to this city and this house after being away two years almost to the day, and not a thing seems to have altered. Everything is in the same place: the leaves on the sidewalk, the rocking chair on the porch, my dog lying by the door....

"Gigi, don't you know who it is? Come here, girl. Come here so I can tell you how much I missed you."

She doesn't lift her head; her eyes look up but she doesn't move. She's in one of her moods, putting on a show, being cranky.

"Come on, Gigi, is that any way to welcome me?"

She puts her ears back and wags her tail feebly. Is she going to recognize me or not? No. She closes her eyes, gives a long sigh, and pretends to fall asleep again. I'm sure it's all an act. She can't have forgotten her mistress, who taught her to sit up and beg and to behave herself.

"Wake up, Gigi! Let's hear a growl. Show your teeth if you like, but do something!"

"Give her time to get used to you," says Maman.

Papa doesn't say anything, just watches and smiles at me; it's his way. Maman is already busy with her pots and pans. They haven't changed with me, still the same happy, welcoming attitude.

"Are you hungry?"

"What do you feel like eating?"

"Your macaroni, Maman!"

It's so good! As though I'd never left home.

"We'll have to celebrate, throw a big party; I want to see everyone all together, a whole houseful of people. Call Tante Rollande, Maman, and Tante Rachel, and Tante Thérèse...the whole family! Say Diane's back in town and has lots to tell them."

No sooner said than done. The visits begin and we start having fun.

"Yves isn't with you? Did you come by yourself?"

"He's driving down. I came by plane."

"How is it we hardly ever see you on TV any more? And we don't hear about you on the radio or in the papers."

I explain my new doctor's orders and insist that nobody spread the news of my arrival in Montreal. But the journalists know already. How do they do it? Have they got antennae? Someone must have recognized me at the airport. I have to admit that with my wheelchair and breathing apparatus I'm not exactly invisible. Someone is asking for me on the telephone and Maman answers according to my instructions:

"No...Diane is in Toronto having some tests done.... What's that? In Montreal? You must have been misinformed. All right, goodbye."

Phew! Several times during my visit the journalists try to reach me. In vain. I'm here for my family and a few close friends and they know how to hold their tongues. My visit will be a closely guarded secret. I talk and talk and sing and laugh. Mama gets out the photo albums and I go over the story of my two-year adventure for my friends. All these memories seem so distant.

"Look here, this is a picture of the Stanford recipients. That's Howard I was telling you about, and that's Roberta who had the transplant instead of me, and there's Gayle, Andrea, John, Monty, and me." Of those seven people only three are still alive. In twenty-three months I saw more people die than lots of people do in a lifetime. But I don't linger, I turn the pages. "Here's Chuck Walker. He's come through two transplants and look at the way he's smiling and enjoying life. Chuck's a winner, and so am I. You'll see, I'll soon be back on my feet, without my oxygen, and I'll be dancing the way I used to. Like in those old photos where I don't look at all ill, when I weighed 102 pounds, before Isabelle was born." I close the album. I feel a little tired. "What if we did something else? Would you like me to play some old favourites for you?"

We move to the living room and the evening ends in song. The whole week goes by flooded with the joy of meeting old friends again and it does me a world of good. It's as though I'm stocking up on friendship for the rest of the winter. At the end of the week I also get to hold my little girl in my arms again; her father has consented to lend her to me for two days. As if I only had a right to a little piece of Isabelle, as if you could measure out a mother's love! So what! "When I'm better, my darling, when I'm finally able to look after you full time, we won't lose a single crumb of our great big happiness."

"Are they soon going to give you your new little heart, Maman?"

"Yes, *mon chou*, it won't be long now."

Another moving experience awaits me towards the end of my visit, one that would make the trip memorable all by itself. As soon as Yves arrives from Toronto, we start making arrangements to meet Ghus. Yves has already gone to see him at the Federal Correctional Centre on an earlier visit to Montreal. However, because of my state of health it would be difficult for me to meet him, as Yves did, in the big, noisy visiting room. I telephone the director of the penitentiary to get special permission to go outside normal visiting hours. This gentleman, who has followed my story in the papers and knows about my correspondence with Ghus, is really in favour of the idea. A few days later Yves and I push through the heavy doors of the prison.

Ghus hasn't been informed; it's a complete surprise for him. When he appears, I share with him the emotion of that incomparable moment when at last two people meet after exchanging letters and photographs. A few seconds' astonishment, a short emotion-charged silence, then an outburst of words and joy and embraces. It's a little like meeting a twenty-eight-year-old brother for the first time—a secret relationship unites us. For three hours we talk of everything under the sun and get rid of all our awkwardness and embarrassment. Yves has told me how little Ghus is like the image people usually have of a convict. I've seen photos of a pleasant, smiling, and very attractive young man. Ghus is more than all that: he is simplicity and generosity itself. I don't dare tell him how impressed I am; he is even more sensitive than his letters gave him out to be. But not at all pretentious. He's certainly out of place here. Luckily he already has the right to short periods of parole without escort, and in a few weeks he'll be entitled to leave for a few hours.

"You know, little sister, I'm sure your liberation is close too."

"Yes, Ghus. I have the feeling that everything is going to go very fast now. I have a feeling that better times aren't too far away."

For the time being, alas, it's time to leave. My oxygen tank is beginning to act up—it's almost empty. We've got to go.

"Goodbye, Ghus!"

"I'll see you again soon, Diane!"

"Yes, I'll be seeing you."

The door closes behind us. Back home again there's the good smell of cooking, and my dog is lying by the door. I bend down and run my hand through her warm fur.

"Listen, Gigi, I've got to go. Be nice to me, just once!"

Suddenly she opens her eyes, springs to her feet, shakes herself, rubs up against my leg. Then she begins studiously licking my fingers. She's recognized me. You'd even say she had a hunch I'd be back soon.

CHAPTER TWENTY-NINE

Providential Friends

October 24–November 24, 1985

It's thanks to Pierrette Côté that we met the Savoies and are temporarily living with them. This warm and welcoming couple often take in Francophones passing through Toronto. They're both New Brunswickers and have kept their rich accent and legendary hospitality. Together they are living out their retirement in harmony, and now that their own children have gone, they're ready to adopt whoever comes along. They have hearts of gold and immediately took me under their wing.

Yves and I share the largest of the three bedrooms in their little house, a room filled with holy pictures and a great collection of statues. Which is as good as to say that I felt perfectly secure here right away. Yves refrained from comment, and didn't make fun of me when I said I wanted to go to mass with Madame Savoie. Anyway, since he's found a job we don't have time to fight any more. He leaves the house very early, before I get up, and gets back so tired at night that he goes to bed almost right after supper. Naturally, after being unemployed for two years it's hard to readapt. But he was really happy to get his first pay-cheque. At last some money earned by the sweat of his brow! Even if the Optimist Club hasn't cut off our expense account, he's very proud to be bringing home the bacon himself. He was beginning to get fed up with being dependent and he's glad to be working with his hands again. Since we don't know how much longer I'll have to wait here, we've decided it would be a good idea to look for a place of our own.

The Savoies' house has a slight disadvantage: there's no bathroom on the ground floor, just upstairs and in the basement. Since I can't negotiate stairs alone, Yves has to carry me when I have to go. Mounting and descending the basement stairs is somewhat less than comfortable because they are very narrow and I have to climb on Yves's back and hang on with my arms round his neck. It's only funny the first time....

So we've found a three-room apartment, small but without a staircase, in a modest high-rise we can move into in December. The tenants are mainly senior citizens so there's nurse service in the building, which might come in handy. While we were visiting the apartment, my new beeper gave me two jolts of hope. It had been so long since I heard that terrifying sound that I really thought my hour had come. But no. False alarm!

After my lightning visit to Montreal I was officially added to Dr. Cooper's list. Since then I've been reporting three times a week to the hospital. Each time I'm measured, weighed, and encouraged to put on some pounds. I also do some easy exercises—walking on a treadmill, and a little light weight-lifting. They've increased my oxygen intake again, up to ten litres a minute. It's the maximum the condenser can produce and the minimum I need. I know I haven't much time left to live with my old heart and lungs. I can see that in the doctors' eyes. I can read it on my body, in the tips of my fingers and the colour of my lips.

That doesn't stop me from making plans. I'm always looking towards the future. I always fix a goal for myself as if it were some kind of lifebuoy. First the move, which should take place soon enough, then Christmas. I'm going to sing at midnight mass. When I went to mass with Madame Savoie I was so thrilled by the sound of the organ that I couldn't resist the temptation to try it. I asked to be carried up to the organ loft and played a few pieces after mass. I sang too. For me church music and hymns are the most beautiful prayers imaginable, and I put my whole heart into them. I was fascinated, carried away by emotion. This is the way I met the members of a choir from one of the French parishes in Toronto, particularly Simone and Jean-Claude, a French couple who have been living here for a dozen years. They became my friends; I introduced them to Yves and now they're his friends too. I never cease to be amazed at how well life takes care of things and makes us meet the right people at just the right time.

Jean-Claude is head chef of a little French restaurant and his schedule leaves him some free time during the day, so he immediately offered to take me to the hospital Mondays, Wednesdays, and Fridays. Taking me also means carting along my wheelchair and my oxygen tanks, as Yves has done so often. But Jean-Claude doesn't spare any pains and even finds time to prepare me nice little meals before leaving for work. Though he doesn't show it, I sometimes have the impression I'm stealing hours from his sleep. I don't like being dependent on my friends, and I was glad to learn that I could get special transportation by bus from the Savoies' to the hospital.

Besides helping us these first weeks and sharing their excellent cuisine with us, Simone and Jean-Claude offered to store our furniture at their place. When we made these new friends we weren't sure we'd ever see the furnishings of our three California apartments again. Since he couldn't bring everything with him, Yves entrusted our things to an Ontario mover, who misplaced them somewhere between San Jose and Toronto. We had almost become resigned to the idea of starting over from scratch, from saucepans to mattresses, when the truck finally arrived. "We've got room in the basement," Simone said. "You can also use the garage," Jean-Claude added. Everything becomes so simple when you've got friends.

I'm spoiled at the Savoies' too, because I'm not the only one to enjoy their hospitality. Jeannine comes from Sudbury and is having her allergies treated at the General. I've become very close to this frail woman thirty years older than I am. Jeannine is sensitive and delicate, gentleness itself. She never raises her voice, never says a reproachful word. She's an angel of patience with me. She's so reticent I sometimes feel I should be protecting her like a younger sister. We spend the days doing crafts. She's taught me how to make three-dimensional montages: you take three identical illustrations and cut them out, then stick them on top of one another, leaving the finest details till last. The more intricate and stylized the subject, the better the effect. I'm fond of doing this kind of precision work that keeps my hands busy and leaves my imagination free. Sitting in the kitchen we spend hours on end chatting and cutting out birds and harlequins. Jeannine is a sister to me, big or little, depending on whether I'm sheltering under her wing or doing some little service for her. It's impossible not to develop a family spirit in a house where such a feeling of solidarity reigns.

Madame Savoie has five sons and two daughters who all come, together with their wives, husbands and children, to pay frequent visits to their parents. They come in turn to find out how I am and offer to help however they can.

In such circumstances how can I feel sad or downcast? I haven't got time to worry about my wobbly health. In the midst of my many activities I barely find more than a moment or two to reflect on the fact that I've outlived the first verdict of my doctors by eight months. Thirty more days till Christmas, when I'll sing midnight mass. Nobody can stop me. Right now I'm frantically getting ready for Simone's birthday. I've just finished a little cut-out montage that came out really well and I'm going to give it to her tonight. Jean-Claude has invited us to dinner. It's always an event to eat at their place and tonight there'll certainly be some gourmet surprise or other. Mmmm! I can tell I'm going to have a great time and put on some weight. There are going to be other people there, I think, so I'll have to look my best. In a minute Yves will carry me up to our room where I'll slip on a dress instead of these eternal leather pants. I want to look elegant. I want people to forget I'm sick, because that's still the best way for me not to think of it.

CHAPTER THIRTY

Ready or Not....

November 25, 1985

8:45 p.m.

As we come in, the telephone is ringing in the Savoies' kitchen. Yves answers. He has just put a big box down in the middle of the living room; it's our buy-early Christmas present, a TV set, still packed in its cardboard box.

"It's for you, Diane," he says, handing me the phone.

He's not acting normal. I can't quite interpret the little signs that usually let me know who's on the line. Who could be calling me on a Monday night? Is it bad news?

"Allo?"

"This is Mel Cohen from the Toronto General Hospital." He's the person in charge of organ retrieval. "We have a compatible donor for you. Can you come around to the hospital as soon as possible?"

I don't flinch. It's a repeat of the scenario that happened several times in California. I have the impression I've dreamed it all before, with slight variations. That's why I ask, without the least sign of emotion:

"Are you sure the donor is compatible?"

He assures me that the measurements have been carefully checked, that the size is right and the tissue composition is identical. So is the blood type.

I hang up. This time I have no doubts. I've heard tell of Mel Cohen and I've even caught a glimpse of him on one of my visits to the hospital. Yves hasn't taken his eyes off me during the few seconds our conversation lasted. He knows. He's waiting for the storm, he's certain I'm not going to take this news without protesting. And sure enough....

"It's not the right time! Why should this be happening tonight of all nights? What's the Big Guy in the sky got against VCRs and television sets anyway? And to think I was so looking forward to singing for him.... Now all my plans are wrecked...the move, midnight mass, everything!"

For several minutes I can't see anything for tears of anger and helplessness. I'm the victim of some immense monster of injustice who has nothing better to do than gleefully sabotage my miserable little plans. Yves doesn't say anything. He takes me in his arms and carries me to our room. He's waiting. Jeannine has come up quietly and is waiting too. They're both here, and I know they're trying to help me, but it's as though I'm all alone, plunged into the depths of my misery. I must get out of there, I have to get out by myself. I touch bottom, gather strength one last time, and surface again....

"I won't go!"

I burst out sobbing, unable to control my rage. Then suddenly I stop. I calm down. Yes, all those words they keep saying over and over, I know them off by heart. I haven't been waiting all this time for this very moment just to refuse it and turn my back on it now.

9:15 p.m.

I've called my parents in Montreal. I'm calmer now but I couldn't hide my disappointment. However, my grumpiness seemed more and more futile as I tried to voice it. I'm beginning to realize what's happening. I put together a few toilet articles and my Walkman in a little bag. No suitcase; I'm coming just as I am. I'm ready. But before I leave I insist on having some pictures taken—with Yves, with Jeannine, with Monsieur and Madame Savoie. I smile at the camera. I want to have these souvenirs of the last hours I spent with my old heart and lungs.

10:00 p.m.

We arrive at the hospital. No endless waiting here as in Stanford; we go straight to the second floor, which is reserved for intensive care units and the operating rooms. I am put into a three-bed room that is being vacated for me. I slip on the regulation gown without a fuss and put myself in the expert hands of the nurses. Blood test, then intravenous in both wrists. Esther is nice; she comes from Nova Scotia and speaks a few words of French. Dr. Todd, a surgeon on the transplant team, comes to see me. He wants to reassure me. He explains how I'll react when I come to in two or three days. "You'll see, when they turn off the respirator you'll be afraid to try out your new lungs. Most patients react like that." Not me! I won't be afraid. The very fact that I'm already thinking about this stage gives me a sense of security. It's as if Dr. Todd is admitting that the operation itself is a small thing, of no importance. I suppose he sincerely believes what he's telling me and has no notion of all the anxious hours he'll spend at my bedside.

10:25 p.m.

I've just spoken to my parents and then called Isabelle. I'm sure everything will go all right now. I've taken a small dose of cyclosporine and vitamin K, the same as at Stanford. "I'm an old hand at pre-transplantation," I told Dr. Todd, and he laughed.

He seems to appreciate my good humour. Before leaving he told me that the operation is scheduled for midnight. Good. Perfect. I won't have much longer to wait! Then Esther swabbed my throat with a yellow liquid like iodine; my gown is covered with it; the wall is splattered too. It seems to be the real thing this time. I tune my Walkman to some quiet music. I feel good.

11:40 p.m.

Yves had left the room when Dr. Todd was examining me and now he reappears, accompanied by Jean-Claude. I'm glad to see them.

"Come on, Jean-Claude, take some pictures."

"Diane, you're a photo freak. By the way, the ones we took yesterday are excellent."

Yesterday was the dinner party for Simone's birthday. I had fun. I think I got a little carried away, playing the organ all evening long. Once I get going I can't stop, it's like a drug with me. "You'll tire yourself out," Simone said. "That's okay, I'll have all day to rest up."

"You know, Jean-Claude, Simone was right. Yesterday I over-did it. This morning at the hospital I couldn't finish my usual exercises. They scolded me and sent me back home to the Savoies'. I never thought today would be the big day."

Jean-Claude seems moved.

"This may seem funny, but I was thinking about you a lot today, as if something was going to happen."

"Well, you see—this is it, and I'm no more nervous than if I were going to the dentist. I'm just sorry I won't be able to sing at midnight mass."

"There'll be other Christmases."

"That's true.... Come on, Yves, take a picture of us like this. That's it! Is the yellow spot on the wall in it?"

"Can't keep it out, Diane."

"Doesn't matter. It'll be more realistic. I'm completely cov-ered myself. Does it look as if I'm about to have a transplant?"

I'm joking and laughing and talking non-stop. But what time is it?

"Wasn't the operation supposed to be at midnight?"

"The operation will be delayed," Mel Cohen tells us. "We have to remove the liver and kidneys from the donor to use in other transplants."

"Three other lives lengthened. That's good! Come here, Yves. Now, Jean-Claude, take a last picture of the two of us."

CHAPTER THIRTY-ONE

Blackout

Yves and Jean-Claude were beside me when I was wheeled away to the operating room at 12:42 a.m. on November 26. They were my two bodyguards, my two guardian angels, two of the three men thanks to whom I can go on with this story. Because a few minutes later I lost consciousness for thirty days. Unfortunately, I don't remember anything about the signs of partial awareness I occasionally showed. For thirty days I was to live an interminable nightmare filled with images that might have come from the worst horror movies. Even if I do remember some of these dreams, most of them are mixed up in my mind with real events. I will mention them when they seem to correspond to my spurts of consciousness. As for the rest, including the facts pertaining to the operation, I have to reconstruct them with the help of my three guardian angels.

First there's my father, who kept a sort of diary in telegraphic style—Papa shows real talent as an archivist. On large sheets of paper, in his fine handwriting, he noted every gesture I made when he was there, the exact time I moved, plus a host of other details he jotted down after telephone conversations with Yves. There are five pages covered front and back with his minuscule writing, pages that have been carefully folded and set aside like precious objects.

Jean-Claude's notes harmoniously complement Papa's news bulletins. He and Simone were my most faithful visitors all during the time I was in intensive care. They spelled my family and particularly Yves, whose patience and constancy were then, and are still, beyond praise. Yves himself is my third and most important informant, and the one who gives meaning to the whole content of this book. I put him through some tough times during the three years this adventure lasted, but none tougher than this period when I hung between life and death. Yves didn't take any notes, but events remained engraved in his memory as indelibly as if I'd written them there myself in letters of blood. The content of what follows is mainly due to his memory.

But at 12:46 I was still completely lucid, despite the powerful drugs I had absorbed intravenously. Yves had stopped to have a word with Dr. Cooper while Jean-Claude continued to walk along beside me towards the operating room. We passed the nurses' station, and I noticed a blackboard with my name written on it in chalk. The donor's name was there too, but I only saw my own.

"There's a spelling mistake. My name is Diane Hébert, not Herbert. Correct it right away."

A nurse stepped up, erased the word, and wrote it properly.

"That's right. Don't forget the accent on the 'e'. Good."

I was satisfied. Jean-Claude smiled at me and gave me a last kiss.

Yves leaned over me. He was wearing the medal I had just given him, the one Jean-Paul Théorêt gave me, which I had never taken off since.

"What were you cooking up with Dr. Cooper?"

"Curious to the last, aren't you, Diane? Dr. Cooper took Jean-Claude for a journalist, the one who tried to pass himself off as your brother. I told him Jean-Claude has become a brother to you."

"It's true. Goodbye, Jean-Claude. See you soon, Yves."

I kissed him tenderly, but already my vision was beginning to blur. I went on moving all alone down the corridor, my stretcher rolling by itself. I'll have to ask them to take more pictures, I thought, mustn't forget to warn the doctors that.... A door opened in front of me and I wouldn't see it close. A door opened, I entered, and plunged into an immense gulf. It was totally dark. Blackout!

Jean-Claude didn't have to insist much to persuade Yves to go and get a bite to eat. There was nothing else to do but wait. That was what he had said to Dr. Cooper a few minutes before: "I've done all I can to get Diane this far; it's up to you to do the rest." "You can count on me," the doctor replied. "And there's no use hanging around here. Go get some rest and think about something else." Jean-Claude and Yves came back about three, accompanied by Simone. Although the operation had begun some time earlier, it wouldn't be finished before morning. Yves decided to stretch out on a couch in a little room beside the waiting room, while Jean-Claude and Simone stood guard.

Dr. Todd was the first to appear, at 6:35.

"Everything's fine," he said. "Everything's going according to plan."

He seemed calm and self-confident. A little later it was Mel Cohen's turn to come and reassure them. The heart and lungs had been removed at 2:10; surgery was proceeding normally. Jean-Claude hurried over to give Yves the good news and then left to take Simone to work. He returned just in time to hear from Dr. Cooper himself that the operation was satisfactory.

It was now 10:20 and Dr. Cooper seemed exhausted, as if he had been through a hard struggle. Jean-Claude observed in his notes that he seemed to be weighing his words, and spoke of a small problem.

"The heart is slightly too large and is rather confined in the thoracic cage. Just the same, Diane should be coming back to her room soon." Yves wasn't especially troubled by this little problem, in fact he was so pleased he decided to go right up to the tenth floor to tell the good news to the nurses who knew me. However, Jean-Claude was less enthusiastic. "If the problem were so small," he wrote in his notebook, "the doctor wouldn't have mentioned it." While Yves gave free rein to his joy, Jean-Claude waited by the elevators.

At 10:50 I was taken from the operating room to my room in intensive care. Jean-Claude saw my stretcher go by and recognized me by my blonde hair. He was reassured too. Yves turned up shortly after.

"I saw Diane," Jean-Claude said in an excited voice. "Everything's all right."

My two friends were ecstatic.

"Come on, let's get some air! Let's celebrate!"

"Yes, I'll call Simone."

But just as they were about to take the elevator, they saw Dr. Cooper rushing out of it and over towards the intensive care unit, presumably to my room. The suspense lasted until 11:45, when Dr. Cooper came over to Yves and Jean-Claude to announce:

"It's a cardiac arrest. She'll have to go back to the operating room."

Consternation.

At 1:00 p.m. Dr. Todd came to confirm what Cooper had said. The blood pressure was too strong. An hour later Dr. Cooper reappeared and this time he seemed vanquished.

"Don't expect too much...the worst may happen. You'd better call her parents."

His heart breaking, Yves phoned my family. Cooper returned to the operating room. My new heart was swollen, it had grown even larger, it was impossible to close the chest cavity. The surgeon decided to improvise and leave the rib cage open, protected only by a film of cellophane.

My condition seemed stable but offered little hope. Everyone's morale was at rock bottom. Yves agreed to go and rest at the Savoies'; he was worn out. And it was there in the solitude of our room that he at last let his body rid itself of all its tensions. Yes, my big strong man broke into tears, the best way to let off steam when the pressure's too strong. After the crisis passed, he showered and came back to the hospital. Cooper was there. He still seemed upset but suggested that Yves come and see me in my room in intensive care.

"Talk to her," he said. "Try to get some reaction from her."

Yves put on the regulation costume: cap, gown, plastic over-shoes (always too small), mask, and gloves. Esther was at my bedside. As soon as she saw him come in she offered him a chair and a glass of water.

"You know, it's sometimes hard to take," she said.

"Don't worry," my stoical friend replied.

He came over to the bed. I was unrecognizable, tied together with tubes and ligatures; there was nothing human about me. My face was swollen and dirty. The sheets and bandages were splotched with blood. Yves turned to Esther:

"If the offer's still good, I'll take that chair and glass of water."

He sat down beside me and held my hand. I didn't react. My eyes were closed and my fingers lay lifelessly in his warm hand. He spoke to me, but I didn't hear.

"Listen, Diane. It doesn't matter if you can't hear me. It's ridiculous, I know, but I'm talking for myself, for my own good. I think the worst is over now, for you as well as for me. But I know you've got to go on fighting with all your strength. Cooper and I did all we could. The rest is up to you. If you can hear me now, I beg you, go on fighting. You've got to win this battle, and you know I know you can. Do what you *want*, Diane."

I didn't react, didn't stir, didn't close or relax my fingers. All Yves could see was the gaping hole in my chest and my heart beating under the cellophane.

No, I didn't hear anything—or if I did I don't remember any more.

CHAPTER THIRTY-TWO

Just One Sign....

It had been an agitated night on the second floor. At 2:45 on November 27, there was a second cardiac arrest and another return to the operating room. My heart was massaged back to life by Dr. Todd. This time Dr. Cooper put in metal clamps to enlarge the chest cavity; then he decided to close it and sew the incision together. My parents, who had now arrived, lived to the full the anguish of these comings and goings to and from the operating room, the surgeons rushing in and out, the interminable hours of waiting. A little later on, another nerve-racking alert: when Jean-Claude called in the morning, everyone's morale was at a new low because there had been a third cardiac arrest caused by blood clots in the arteries. When, oh when would they invent a surgical zipper? The chest cavity had to be opened and cleaned again. As for my lungs, they were performing normally—no trouble on that score.

In the waiting room morale rose and fell to the rhythm of my heart-beat. From the gloom of late afternoon it climbed slightly in the evening, particularly after a visit from Mary, Toronto's fourth heart-lung transplant. "She's so frail," Jean-Claude wrote in his journal, "and yet there she is before us. Therefore every-thing is possible, and we must never stop believing and hoping." "Every minute that passes," he added, "is a minute gained."

This relatively calm closing to the first day was disturbed by the arrival of the journalists. Who gave them the news? It remains a complete mystery. But there they were anyway, like a cloud of hornets, on the lookout for the latest rumour, spying on the doctors' movements, pacing the hospital corridors. They questioned my parents and clicked their indiscreet cameras at them. When Yves caught on to their game, he saw red and let them have it, ordering them politely but firmly to leave. The unsympathetic brutes wouldn't budge. It took Dr. Cooper's fury and the arrival of a few hefty reinforcements to disperse the inquisitive band. Jean-Claude was struck by their boldness too. "What could we have told them?" he asks in his notes. "Diane's condition changes so rapidly. What we tell them tonight could very well be completely false by the time of the morning papers." Yes, my condition was far from stable, but it looked to Yves and Jean-Claude, who had decided to stick around and spell my parents, as though the evening might be a little calmer.

The waiting room of the intensive care unit was the scene of terrible anxieties. Family and friends of other patients were subjected to the same awful uncertainty. One of these was Gilles, a young man from Lac St-Jean who was going through a most painful ordeal. His twenty-two-year-old wife had failed to regain consciousness after surgery performed in Quebec to allay cancer of the larynx. She had been transferred to Toronto and put under the care of the best specialists, but they hadn't been able to bring her around either, and she remained hanging between life and death. Gilles didn't speak English, and since he was alone he soon became friends with Yves and Jean-Claude. Others in similar circumstances joined this little group, sharing the fear and anguish of the relapses, and incomparable relief when things improved. It was an abruptly changing, unforeseeable rhythm, like the one every human being is subject to over a lifetime, but in this case condensed in time and harder to bear. And in sharing these strong emotions everyone had to fall back on his or her own resources and reasons for hope.

That night, shortly after supper, Yves was alone in the waiting room, when Dr. Cooper came in. Gilles had gone out and Jean-Claude was not due until later that evening. Dr. Cooper seemed exhausted. He slumped in an armchair and put his feet up on the low table littered with magazines. For once he seemed ready to abandon his cold, severe attitude. The two men chatted a little together before broaching the subject that most concerned them. Joel Cooper was surprised at the way things had turned out and admitted that he had underestimated my powers of resistance.

"I didn't think she was so tough, so stubborn," he said. Yves told him he'd never doubted my doggedness.

"Now we have to make her react," Cooper said. "Go and see her, talk to her, make her give you a sign. I can't hide from you the fact that all this surgery may have caused some brain damage."

Yves was shaken. "I'll try," he said.

He got up and followed the doctor into the intensive care unit. He put on the obligatory costume and came into my room. A nurse was sitting by the bed. I was still surrounded by all sorts of machines and my appearance hadn't improved. Yves sat down and took my hand.

"Diane, I'm here and I know you can hear me, so prove it to me. Give me a sign. I know it's going to cost you an enormous effort, but take your time, I'm not in any hurry. I'm going to wait here just as long as you want."

He kept on endlessly repeating the same thing: "Move your fingers. Open your eyes. Squeeze my hand. Do you feel the warmth of my palm?"

Yves is the soul of patience. He could have kept on like that for hours. But I didn't want to keep him waiting; I felt his hand on mine, warm and alive, so I gently closed my fingers.

Yves couldn't contain his joy.

"She did it, Dr. Cooper! She closed her fingers, she squeezed my hand, she knows what she's doing!"

He told me later he had never seen Dr. Cooper so moved.

CHAPTER THIRTY-THREE

Nothing Gained

Every day my least movements were interpreted as signs of improvement. Thursday I opened my eyes for the first time. The next day it was my parents' turn to put on the visitors' uniform and sit beside me. "We saw her this morning and she understood us," Papa wrote on November 29. But barely thirty hours after their visit I was taken back to the operating room. One of the clamps was starting to tear the skin and there was blood in my lungs. By 9:20 Saturday evening I was back in my room again, however, and spent a good night. The state of my health continued to cause alarm, even though I was recuperating quickly. At all times I was in a very precarious condition; the four operations had weakened me and I weighed only seventy pounds. Yet I was staying awake for several minutes at a time now and showing distinct signs of understanding. Jean-Claude came to see me for the first time; until then he had only looked through the glass of my "aquarium" as I lay there in a jumble of machines and tubes.

"She understands what I say," he wrote, "and tries in vain to speak. But who in the world could speak intelligibly with a tube between her lips, another in her nose, the whole thing strapped on by adhesive tape? Still, we try to communicate; I have to invent questions she can answer by yes or no. I hold her hand and she recognizes me by the sound of my voice, for she has trouble opening her eyes. Despite the pleasure that registers on her face, I can sense that her body is ceaselessly fighting and suffering."

Jean-Claude was right; I never stopped fighting and suffering. I just have to remember some of my dreams to see that I was engaged in a fierce combat against death. I suppose the drugs I was given increased the horror of those visions. I was beset by all kinds of monsters. Strangely enough, in my dreams the nurses were my worst enemies; they worked against me. They were either trying to poison me or plotting to steal my body and remove it far from the doctors' care. It was probably their continual presence at my bedside that made me cast them as the principal villains in the scenario of my delirium. I could recognize their faces perfectly and completely in my dreams, although in reality I could only see their eyes above the protective masks. I suppose that in some way I had to transpose the permanent pain I was suffering, and that my subconscious found nothing better than to accuse them of being my torturers.

Subtler minds may find other interpretations. Maybe I wished to give myself up to death, to refuse any help from people who would prolong my suffering. That could be, but as a hypothesis it sets aside the hours, days, and years I held so vigorously to life. Besides, when Jean-Claude said to me before leaving, "Don't give up, Diane. Hang in there! We're all with you!" I would nod my head in agreement. Who could claim with any certainty that this gesture was only dictated by my instinct for self-preservation? The one sure thing is that the battle was joined. I *willed* myself to live!

CHAPTER THIRTY-FOUR

A Day-to-Day Struggle

(From Jean-Claude's journal)

December 3. Today Diane opened her eyes wide. At last we can see her luminous gaze resting on us a little longer. It reminds me of what she said when Dr. Todd warned her about certain post-operative difficulties. "It will be hard for you to talk," he said. "That doesn't matter, I've got my eyes—they'll talk for me," she replied. And it's true.

She is so wide awake and restless they've had to tie her hands to prevent her from touching the machines around her. She moves a lot and lifts her arms towards her chest. She seems to be asking me to explain why she's attached to so many tubes. I try to calm her down, saying we'll talk about it when she's feeling better. For the first time they sat her up in bed for about ten minutes. Everything seems to be a new experience for her.

December 4. Diane was moving around a lot when I went to see her as usual just after work. Again we had to tie her hands to the bars of her bed. She was trying to pull out one of the tubes. How vigilant the nurses have to be, and how patient, and how considerate they are! But Diane is very crafty. She manages to turn on her side and bend her head towards her hand so she can grab the tube. Her brain is very sharp and she's using it well. I have to speak to her a little roughly (and it's not easy): "Be still, Diane, and don't touch that tube! Promise me, now." She nods yes but at the same time tries to grab it again. I look at her scoldingly and she looks back making a face as if to say, "Yes, I know, big brother, but if you only knew how sick I am of this tube!" How well I understand her!

Today Diane's face is decidedly less swollen. Last week she got all her colour back but you could barely recognize her pretty features. I tell her that she's looking beautiful and that seems to please her. It even earns me a smile from among the tubes.

The first smile, the first word, the first movement. I was just like a newborn baby. Is that why my memory has been playing tricks on me?

December 5. If Jean-Claude was my most faithful visitor, Yves was practically part of the hospital staff. He came several times a day, asked about my least gestures, followed my progress enthusiastically. Dr. Cooper suggested that he bring some things that were important to me. "It's not enough to make her react, we must also provide her with opportunities for motivation. Bring her some objects she's particularly attached to. That will stir happy memories and help her continue the fight."

So my man brought in photos and letters. I was sleeping when he came in, and he waited till I opened my eyes. I was happy to find him near me; I moved around, wriggled in bed. And I was looking better. Yves talked to me as usual and told me what time it was, the date and the day of the week, to help me get my bearings. I listened without displaying much interest. Then he showed me the photos, pictures of Isabelle. My hands weren't tied; I grabbed the photos and then shoved them violently away. "What's the matter, Diane, don't you recognize Isabelle?"

I had tears in my eyes. I nodded my head, took the photos back, and hugged them to my heart. Yves let me be, took an envelope out of his pocket and began to read a letter from Ghus. I repeated the same gesture—snatched the letter from him and crushed it to my heart with the photos. Then I remained motionless a few moments. Only my eyes moved, shifting from Yves to the door—first to Yves, then to the door. He didn't understand. I freed one of my hands from the photos and pointed to the door. Yves went on saying he didn't follow me. Then my eyes began to throw out sparks: anger, despair, pleading. I pointed to the door again, then to Yves, then to me. I did it all over in reverse order: pointed to myself with the letters and the photos, to myself with Yves, then the door.

It was simple: "I'm sick of this bed and this hospital. I want to leave."

December 6. I'm leaving. What a relief! I'm being wheeled out of here on a bed. I feel fine. But suddenly I realize why I'm being taken away. They want to steal me. It's a plot. I'm being transferred to another hospital where the staff are all nurses. They hold me prisoner and demand a ransom. They want all my money. I explain that I haven't got a cent on me. "Let me telephone Yves, he'll send some."

They accept. They stand beside me while I dial the number. It's okay, they don't understand French so I can tell my man they've kidnapped me and he'll have to get here fast. He's come. He's with a group of doctors. They've had the great idea of passing themselves off as purchasers of the hospital. They pretend to be interested in the condition of the building and investigate it inside out. Unfortunately they pass right by the room I'm locked up in. It's a laboratory where corpses are dissected, just like Frankenstein's castle. I'm stretched out on the table and they want to remove my brain. Rita comes closer with a needle in her hand....

"Yves!"

He was there leaning over me, but he wasn't holding a needle.

December 7. I was feverish, and that worried the doctors. Dr. Todd and Dr. Cooper regularly consulted my most devoted companion.

"How do you find her?" they asked Yves.

"Calmer. More passive. But I've noticed that her eyes are yellow today. Could there be something wrong with her liver?"

Our nearest and dearest ones' observations are often worth as much as the experts' when it comes to tracking down problems. I was examined again on the operating table. Gall bladder, liver, and lungs were all right, but the pancreas was slightly swollen, probably due to my diet, so the doctors regulated and varied my liquid menu. As for my heart, it seemed to be adapting well to its new space, and my blood pressure had stabilized. This was excellent news. However, as an additional precaution the volume of my chest cavity had to be maintained at a maximum. The doctors had improvised a system of wires, pulleys, and weights to take the weight off my sternum.

December 8. I was terribly frustrated not to be able to make myself heard. However eloquent my eyes might be, they couldn't say everything. That morning Yves brought me a board with all the letters of the alphabet on it. I caught on immediately: He wanted me to point out letters to spell words. I showed him E, then A, then T. I took the cake for a fast learner, letting him know I was hungry—not bad for a baby! Naturally, there was no question of feeding me normally. Yves brought me little bits of flavoured ice to suck on. Because of that horrible tube I had in my mouth, it wasn't easy, but I managed. D-E-L-I-C-I-O-U-S.

December 9. As might be expected, after being fed, I felt the urge to go. "I want to go to the bathroom," I said by my board. Yves teased me gently: "You've got a catheter," he said. I was furious; I understand babies' rages better and better.

December 10. Breathing exercises and biopsy. They'd taken down the wires, pulleys, and weights. Every machine they removed was a sign of progress. "And the tubes? What use are they?" I asked. Yves didn't seem to have any idea how uncomfortable they were.

December 11. I tried to pull out the one that went up my nose. In vain—the nurses had eyes in the backs of their heads. None the less, I'd begun to breathe by myself. But I was terribly afraid to rely on my new lungs. I took tiny little breaths and didn't get rid of enough carbon dioxide. As a result my blood didn't have enough oxygen. Dr. Todd was right—it's a source of untold anguish to have to count on new lungs. It was as though I didn't trust them.

December 12. Biopsy. I'm in the basement of Simone and Jean-Claude's house. I'm spread out on the washing machine in the laundry room. My friends are upstairs with Yves. Dr. Todd is with me. He's not going to hurt me. "You won't feel a thing," he says. It's a good dream. I wish it would last for ever.

December 14. Every day they came in to weigh me. It was the time I dreaded most in the whole day. They lifted me up in bed by means of a kind of stretcher I had to roll onto. My poor body was nothing but skin and bone. It was immensely painful. I dreamed I was stretched out on my back, hands and arms strapped above my head, and they were making my body pivot around a post at dizzying speed. It made me sick to my stomach.

December 15. Little by little they were increasing the length of time I had to breathe on my own. That day it was half an hour. It tired me out terribly. Nobody seemed to notice. You'd have said the doctors weren't aware of the superhuman effort I was making. I was sick of it!

December 16. I didn't want to see anybody. What were they doing, trying to finish me off? Did they think it was easy to be reborn? Get out! You, too, Dr. Cooper! But he didn't hear a thing. Was it on purpose that he took away my voice? I showed him the door, pointing at it. He pretended not to understand. He wouldn't go. How pig-headed can you be! If looks could kill...! He smiled at me.

"Listen carefully, Diane, I'm very pleased with your progress. Tomorrow if everything goes well, we can turn off the respirator...."

Oh! I would have shouted for joy if I'd been able to. Yes, yes, take the tube out, can't you do it right now? Oh, I'll do anything, anything at all to please you, you're so kind, Dr. Cooper, so very, very kind....

December 17. No more tube! At least not that one, the most uncomfortable one, the one I tried to pull out so many times. It was a red-letter day, three weeks exactly after my transplant. "Her expression is radiant," Jean-Claude noted in his journal.

December 18. A dream that recurred often. *I'm hung up like the chassis of an automobile over an assembly line. Nurses look at me wickedly and refuse to let me down. Stop the machines! Unhook me! I can't stand it any more!* "A day without problems," wrote Jean-Claude.

December 19. Papa wrote, "She's breathing by herself but not talking. It's strange, as though her vocal chords were crushed. But she's doing fine." And yet I never ceased screaming in my dreams. Didn't anybody hear me?

December 20. Yves and I arrive on an island by plane. We stop to eat at a little restaurant. A group of doctors and nurses arrives. They greet Yves but ignore me. "Watch out, Yves, they pretend to be your friends but they want to hurt me." My man won't listen. The doctors keep on talking to him while the nurses drag me off to the kitchen in the back. They tie me to a table and Rita comes up to give me a needle. She wants to poison me. Help!

"Were you dreaming?" Dr. Todd asked.

I was glad to see him. I didn't want him to leave.

"There's been a small problem," he said. "We've had to perform a tracheotomy. The liquid in your stomach could have backed up into your lungs. It's over now. The danger's past."

What was he talking about? Was he telling me I'd had a fifth operation? What was this tube coming out of my throat?

"Just be quiet now. Try to get some sleep."

Sleep? Go back to that island with the terrifying nurses?

December 21. It seems I was still very confused and my moments of lucidity were too few. There was a special prescription for this: I must watch my favourite TV series, *The Young and the Restless.* With great effort I tried to keep my eyes open and to show an interest in the lives of these characters on the screen. "Today you only slept fifteen minutes during the show," Yves told me. Sure, I was just closing my eyes for the commercials.

December 22. Yves brought me photos of Isabelle stuck onto a piece of cardboard; he wanted to decorate the room. I refused. I was too afraid someone would steal them. I didn't trust the nurses. Besides, I didn't want my daughter to see me that way. I saw my face in the mirror and I didn't recognize myself. I looked awful. I didn't like myself. Let me sleep in peace!

December 23. Papa wrote: "Diane was sitting up when we came in. An aide washed her hair. I dried it for her."

I don't remember. Yet I seemed to understand when Maman talked about Christmas and midnight mass. Yes, I wanted to sing at the Church of the Sacred Heart with Simone and Jean-Claude. But something happened. What am I doing in this bed?

CHAPTER THIRTY-FIVE

Awakening

None of the moments of consciousness referred to in the preceding pages left any impression on my memory. Yves, Jean-Claude, and my parents witnessed the first gestures of my rebirth and told me about them so vividly afterwards that I sometimes have the impression I remember a few details. But the flashes of lucidity remain as vague as episodes in my earliest childhood. My thirty-day amnesia is a black gulf traversed only by dreams. When Yves and I recall this foggy period together and I try to put a little order into it, he often says, "No, Diane, you didn't dream that, you really experienced it. That big tube they put through your nose into your lungs was for a bronchoscopy. It's thanks to that examination that you ended up having the tracheotomy, which helped you a lot."

Good. If I've forgotten it, so much the better. I suppose my memory looked after sorting out events, and chose to keep the most pleasant ones. Maybe that's why I recall Christmas Eve as my first real memory, as if I had just awakened from a long night's sleep. Maybe I unconsciously chose this date because of the happy, holiday feelings it evoked. I don't know. But it was really like opening my eyes for the first time.

December 24, 1985

The room is small and dark. Near the built-in wash basin is a messy countertop with a lot of little bottles on it. There's a clock on the white wall that says 7:20—morning or evening? I try to figure out where the window is. There isn't one. There's a lot of noise in my ears, a constant, irritating, bubbling sound. I see, it's the machines. Turning my head I can see a console of some kind, with lots of knobs and a tangle of wires coming out of it. I'm in bed lying on my back. I don't try to get up. I don't think I'd be able to. Anyway, I don't want to. It's a little as though I don't feel my body. Am I dead? No, I can move; I can lift my hand and touch my mouth. My hand is very thin, I've never seen it so small. My wrist has a hole in it and is attached to a big wire that moves when I do. My arm is covered with brown hairs. I remember, it's due to the cyclosporin, a side-effect. That's what it is—I've had my transplant. My face must be covered in fuzz too. Yes, my fingers touch the hairs, they're soft but not at all like peach fuzz. And my cheeks are swollen. But I'm breathing...I've got new lungs, and undoubtedly a new heart. So the mechanism has been changed....

What's this tube coming out of my throat? Oh! There's someone sitting beside me, it must be a nurse. It's a woman, in any case, and she has pretty hands, long, well-trimmed nails; she's taking notes in a book. Is she wicked? Is she going to torture me? I hope not. She turns around. Someone else has just come into the room. I can only see his eyes, brown eyes I recognize immediately—it's Yves. *Yves!* I try to speak but I can't. *Yves!* He smiles at me. What do I look like? I must look awful. I touch my hair; it's silky. They've just combed it. Yes, I can read in his eyes that he still finds me beautiful. He comes over. He's carrying a little box wrapped up in red paper. A present? I smile at him. He speaks to me gently.

"Merry Christmas, Diane! I'm a bit ahead of time, but I've bought you a little something. If you like, I'll open it for you."

No. I shake my head vigorously from right to left. I implore him with my eyes: no, I want to open it myself. He understands. He rolls the table to me, cranks up the bed. There's a pain in my chest, it's cramped in there. I think: "A new heart. New lungs. At last!" The little box is there in front of me in its shiny paper. I'm going to unwrap it. I haven't forgotten how. My movements are clumsy; my hands tremble terribly. Quick now! I tear back the paper, pry at the lid, at last the box is open. What is it? Oh! It's soft, it's white, it's smooth...a ball, another, it's a little man, a snowman. It's pretty, it's lovely! Yves takes it in his hand for a second and puts it down on the table again. I hear a little tune. A Christmas carol, I think. Yes. Oh, how wonderful! I've never heard sweeter music. But tears begin to prick at my eyes. All of a sudden I'm sad, sad and ashamed.

"What's the matter, Diane? You're crying. Aren't you pleased?"

Pleased? I'm so unhappy! I toss in my bed—I want to speak, to tell him. Yves's eyes have shadowed, he's terribly disappointed.

"I know it's not much, but I chose it myself, I thought you'd like it...."

The tears keep coming. I try to speak again but only a sob issues from my mouth, an inaudible and despairing moan.

"Diane, why are you crying?"

I make an effort and manage to articulate: "Oh, Yves! But I haven't got anything for you!"

CHAPTER THIRTY-SIX

Time Stands Still

December 25. I've got another present, this time from the doctors. I'm moving, leaving intensive care. Yves tried to collect my things in the little bag they provided for this purpose. Much too small, their little bag! In my moments of lucidity I've asked family and friends for a whole lot of indispensable things: underwear, stockings, a dressing gown and slippers, my vanity case bulging with make-up, and an electric game that allows me to write whatever I want. All that plus quite a few presents, among them the musical snowman, had to be carried in a big green garbage bag. An overzealous janitor picked it up and threw it out with the trash—at least, that's what must have happened, because I never saw anything again. As far as Christmases go, I've seen better. But let that pass.

It's a very large room on the eleventh floor with two big windows. I'm spoiled. I still have twenty-four-hour nursing care. I've no regrets at leaving the team on the second floor. According to Yves, I owe a great deal to those devoted, patient women who, besides watching over me day and night, washed me and wiped me and kept me clean in exemplary fashion. Real angels, that's what he calls Esther, Lewis, Elizabeth, and Rita—the very same nurses who filled my demonic nightmares. I must admit that the grudge I hold against them is beginning to diminish. I suppose that in time it will disappear completely and I'll be able to show them the gratitude they deserve. Of course, my man was able to get close to them and observe their competence first-hand. They had a thankless task, stopping me from pulling my tube out and putting up with my exasperation. Once, just once, I escaped their vigilance, and the result is a scar on my right cheek as wide as the adhesive paper that was holding my respirator.

Here, on the contrary, I'm treated almost like an ordinary patient. No more machines, with the exception of the one that measures the concentration of oxygen in my blood; it's attached to my toe by a wire. I've still got the tracheotomy tube stuck in my throat with the oxygen mask planted on it. It's not too disagreeable, no more than the one that comes out of my nose that is used to feed me. No, I still can't stuff myself with *tourtière* and turkey the way Maman, Papa, Yves, and his parents are doing. Which is why I find the time so long. At least twenty times today I've opened my eyes and stared at the date on the calendar. It's still December 25. Time stands still.

Yves came to see me, then Maman, then Jean-Claude, one after the other. They don't have to disguise themselves as microbes any more, and don't have to wear masks. Papa came too. I pointed out letters on my board spelling W-A-S-H-C-L-O-T-H, a long word to write. He understood before I finished. Papa is so kind. It really did me good, especially my mouth; my lips are like sandpaper. Then he left too. Too soon! I close my eyes. Ah, if only the day would end. As I said, I've seen better Christmases.

December 26. The date has changed but everything else is still the same. I feel washed out, very tired. Where is the nurse? There she is near the sink, getting my food ready, in a manner of speaking: drops from one little bottle, then from another bottle, then from a third. Not exactly appetizing! I'm not hungry anyway, just thinking about food makes me queasy. I haven't the heart for it. What a strange expression! For that matter I can't feel my heart, they've "denerved" it. Dr. Cooper explained that to me. If I have a heart attack I won't suffer. So much the better! I'll die without pain. Ah, but it's not true! I really do feel sick to my stomach. As for eating—ugh! I don't want anything. Just let me sleep.

December 27. Who changed the numbers? Who changed the date? She or he must have been mistaken. It's at least twelve days that I've been looking at the number twenty-seven. Jean-Claude came, then Maman, then Papa. He stayed a little but not long. Not long enough! When he wanted to go I said *already*? with my lips. *Stay!* I cried. He didn't leave right away but I shut my eyes. Then they took me down to a floor below for a biopsy and brought me back to my room again. Papa and Maman came, then left. I was washed. A cat-wash, a little bit at a time. The arms, the stomach, the legs, the rest. I like it better when Yves washes me, but he didn't come. He's not feeling well. My parents came and went. And it's still the twenty-seventh, the twenty-seventh, the twenty-seventh....

December 28. Today it's better. Papa and a nurse helped me sit up in an armchair, and I could see the snow through the window. I did leg exercises. A little later Yves came and I sat in my armchair again, but I was very tired. He says it's normal, it's an enormous effort but I mustn't stop because of that, and I should try walking as soon as I can. He doesn't seem to know how difficult it is—even to sit up.

December 29. I walked as far as the nurses' station, a distance of a hundred feet, with the help of a metal walker on wheels. My first steps! I'm pleased but exhausted.

December 30. Today's great event is my first bath. Sheer heaven! It's really the nicest thing that has happened to me for a long time, since my rebirth. I could spend my life in the bathtub, stretched out in the warm water. I was ecstatic, as exuberant as a baby.

What a wonder water is! And a bath is miraculous. I'm sure I appreciate even the simplest pleasures more now. It wouldn't take much for me to say that this bath was worth all the suffering I've gone through. But I'll be more prudent and just say, "*Vive la nature!* Long live plumbers!"

December 31. It's fantastic! I've almost lost the fear of breathing. Pump away, heart. Get pink, lungs. I'm alive. Today I don't want to sleep, I want to make myself beautiful. I've asked to have my "first aid" kit brought to me: my make-up and manicure set. I cut and filed my nails by myself. They're growing well now and have never been stronger. It's a positive side-effect of the cyclosporin; before they were soft and always breaking. I won't bite them any more. I'll have pretty hands like real women. I've always thought beauty should be visible to the ends of one's fingertips. My hair has changed too, from blonde to brown. That's perfect—it'll match my eyes.

My eyes are still my strong point; I have long, full lashes and thick, silky eyebrows. The rest of my face is rather spoiled: swollen cheeks, fuzzy skin, lips chapped and dry. Bah! That'll all come right again, I've seen enough transplants to know that such handicaps are only temporary. For the time being I'm going to work on my eyebrows and give them back their true natural line. When my visitors come, I'll be radiant, sitting back in my bed, smiling.

We'll look at photos together and they'll answer all my questions. I want to know everything the doctors did, every last one of their actions. I don't want to be in the dark about a single aspect of my resurrection. I want to hear Papa say when he leaves, "Today was your best day." Yes, I want to gather my strength for the new year beginning tomorrow—a year as new as my heart and lungs.

CHAPTER THIRTY-SEVEN

Forward, March!

January 11, 1986

Every day marks some tangible progress over the day before. In less than two weeks they've removed my three remaining tubes one by one, so that I'm beginning to eat, drink, and evacuate normally. In short, I am now going through the stages of a standard convalescence almost like any other patient. I can almost believe that the worst is over, that the little bit of journey left to travel will be the sweetest. I would dearly like to nurse the illusion that my new life offers me the excitement of a whole series of first discoveries. But it's not so. I do indeed feel like a child before a bathtub full of water, but I have not the slightest desire to cross the corridor to get there. Standing drains me. Walking is a painful ordeal. Even getting up seems to be an act of pure masochism. It feels as though my bones are fractured into thousands of little pieces that threaten to crumble as soon as I want to make them move. I imagine my insides as a huge jigsaw puzzle that someone is trying to hold up vertically. What a hope! I'm certainly going to collapse.... No, it's sticking together. Thank goodness for the walker! Now, lift one heavy, trembling leg, thrust it ahead of the other, and put it down. That may seem easy to do, and really it is, but it's infinitely painful.

"Just one more little walk, Diane, from here to the nurses' station. Come on, it's not far, a hundred feet at the most."

"No, Yves, I'm tired."

"Come on, Diane, one extra trip every day. You have to do it. Lean on me. I'll help you."

"But I can't go on...."

"Just one more, Diane, and I'll bring you back in the wheelchair."

"No!"

I feel like a dog they're trying to train. If this goes on they'll be giving me a lump of sugar after every trip down the corridor. I'd prefer a little package of salt to perk up the flavour of the insipid food I have to ingest every day. A saltless diet and the daily promenade are the only obligations I have. If only I could see a little improvement, some slight strengthening of my leg muscles.... But no, the fifth lap is as difficult as the first. And afterwards I'm so exhausted I just want one thing: to lie down again.

"I know everything you're feeling, Diane. I lived through the same frustrations and the same hesitations. You get the impression you're tiring yourself out for nothing. Or worse, that the effort you're making is slowing down your recovery. But I know for a fact it's not true. On the contrary, what seems hardest to bear now is exactly what's going to give you strength. The fight's not over, Diane, there's a long hill left to climb, but the view from the top is worth it—and the sense of victory is priceless."

The woman talking to me is Mary, Toronto's Number Four. She's the only one who can really evaluate my efforts. Beside her, Yves is like an athlete's trainer, only preoccupied with performance levels. So our quarrelling started up again as soon as I could muster a trickle of voice. Oh, it's not much more than a timid breath, a hoarse kind of whisper, but it's better than all the pencils in the world for expressing my desires and, if necessary, my anger.

"Yves, pass me that glass of water on the table."

"Get it yourself, Diane, all you have to do is stretch out your arm."

"I'm tired. Give it to me, Yves."

"Listen, you've got to make an effort. It's good for you. Your parents spoiled you too much, Diane. They do everything for you; they never refuse you anything; they overprotect you. It's very bad for your rehabilitation. You've begun to count on them for the smallest things, things you could very well do yourself. Do you think they're at your beck and call? Can't you see they're making you lazy?"

I don't have time to answer because Maman and Papa come in just then. The glass of water stays on the table. We chat a few minutes, then I lean forward, and when I stretch out my arm towards the glass Papa is there before me, hurrying to reach it. Yves tries to prevent him, makes a clumsy move, and the water spills all over me. I'm furious.

"You did it on purpose. You wanted to soak me!"

"Not at all. I wanted you to get it yourself!"

"That's not true! Anyway, I've had enough of you. You're always bullying me. Get out! I don't want to see you any more!"

"But, Diane, you don't understand...."

"You're the one who doesn't understand. Go away! I don't want anything more to do with you!"

Yves leaves in a huff. I cry and cough. Maman lets fly some choice reproaches, which for once I agree with entirely. My parents have never been wildly enthusiastic about Yves, and I usually serve more or less as a buffer between them. I think it's all due to the different ways they show their love for me, my parents trying to anticipate my wishes, Yves trying to reason with me.

Out of respect for their modesty, I've given my parents a very secondary role in this story. Although they weren't present at every stage of my ordeal, they never failed to give me their moral support—and on occasion, financial support too. From the moment they became aware of my sickness, they added a good dose of self-sacrifice to their feeling of tenderness for me. They did without things for my sake, and allowed their little routines to be upset. They put up with my furniture in their basement and living room, looked after my dog, went without holidays sometimes, and lived three years of anguish, amplified by distance. That may seem natural to some people, and I know there were times when I too accepted their concern with a pinch of indifference. At the risk of making them blush, I'd say they were perfect parents. And it's surely because they sugar-coated the pill that I managed to swallow it down so easily. I can see how their behaviour could annoy Yves. Close witnesses are sometimes poor judges of love. I'm in no position to defend anyone; I enjoy Papa's little attentions and Maman's devotion too much, and I appreciate Yves's stimulation, too. But I must say that at this particular moment I feel my companion has gone too far. He has—pardon the pun—added the drop that made the cup spill over.

"He needs a holiday," declares Papa, always the diplomat.

"I wish he'd go away for ever! And never come back!"

When I think about the incident later, I understand Yves's exasperation better. For three years we were so close that we shared every instant's anxiety, from those first minutes of waiting to the agonizing hours in intensive care. I can almost say that he lived the whole experience by proxy, he participated in every phase of my transplant so closely. And now he finds himself at exactly the same point as I am: the worst is perhaps over, but the best remains to be won. Life on the eleventh floor isn't lived at the same palpitating rhythm as it was on the second. The close association with the nurses and the relaxed conversations with the doctor are things of the past. I've reverted to the banal status of ordinary patient, and Yves is now just a simple visitor. No more *laisser-passers,* no more privileges. He can barely obtain the right to slightly more flexible visiting hours.

189

Having praised the competence of the Toronto General staff, we now have something to complain about. Nobody seems to pay attention to my real needs, which are often passed off as pure whim. For example, that bottle of mouthwash Yves had to go and get at the drugstore because they claimed there wasn't any in stock.

"You don't mean to tell me that there's not a single bottle left in the hospital?"

No, it's not a caprice on my part. I absolutely need this mixture to cleanse my mouth after coughing up pulmonary secretions. That's one unpleasant effect of having a lung transplant: you have to get rid of all this bitter phlegm. Yves knows it—how many times has he watched me retching the stuff up? To take my side and see that I'm respected, he has to raise his voice in protest. In the circumstances I can't honestly object because I know that his impatience, whether it's directed against me or not, always flares up in order to help me some way or other, even if I don't always appreciate it....

Anyway I'm not one to hold a grudge. After I've chewed over my anger for a few hours, I'm ready to take him in my arms again. He comes back a little sheepishly, full of excuses. There! Isn't that proof of guilt? Perhaps his clumsiness *was* premeditated?

"Promise you won't do it again?"

"Do what again? Oh, the glass of water. Okay, I promise I'll never throw a glass of water in your face again, on one condition...."

"What's that?"

"That you come and take a walk down the hall with me."

"Oh, no! You're just starting all over again!"

"Come on, Diane, just a short walk...."

"I know you. After that it'll be another one."

"No, just one. I promise."

"All right then. Pass me the pen and paper on the windowsill."

"Why?"

"I'm tired of talking. I want to write my answer."

190

Yves turns towards the window, stretches out his hand, hesitates....

"You'd better get it yourself."

I think *you beast*, but I don't say anything. I sit on the edge of the bed, my bones cracking all over. It hurts. Tears come to my eyes, but I hold them back. I put one foot on the floor, then the other. It's only two steps to the window. I grab the paper and the pen, come back to my bed, and sit on it. My hand trembles as I write. My printing is like a child's. Yves comes over to look. I've written two big wobbly letters: NO.

CHAPTER THIRTY-EIGHT

The Price of Glory

January 17, 1986

A few days ago, at the end of a routine visit, Dr. Cooper said, "We're having a little party for you next Friday. If you like, you can invite your 'friends'."

"My friends?"

"Your friends the journalists."

He was smiling. Well, well, I said to myself, Dr. Cooper must be very pleased with "his success" if he's finally consenting to present her to the media. I must have been smiling pretty broadly myself, for he hastily added, "Let's not overdo it, just the same. Two or three at the most."

"All right." Yet it seemed difficult to me to invite only three— that would mean one from radio, one from TV, and one from the newspapers. What about the others? What about those others who followed all the ups and downs of my adventure, wouldn't they be offended? So I didn't really feel I was disobeying Dr. Cooper when I invited six, two from each of the media. It seemed eminently reasonable considering the interest I continue to stir up. The news of my operation has naturally spread far and wide, and people are burning with curiosity to know the details. But I'm afraid I was being extremely naive. You can't divide the world of journalism up this way; in such over-informed circles, if I may use the term, nothing travels faster than news, and now there are a great many of them waiting for me in the corridor of the eleventh floor.

With a shaky hand I give a last touch to my newly styled hair. The cut pleases me; it diminishes the roundness of my cheeks. My clothes are too big; I'm floating in my pants. Will they notice? Bah! Who cares? I'm ready!

Painfully, holding on to the walker, I manage to hoist myself upright. Will my legs hold? I'm terribly afraid they'll let me down—they're not solid at all, and they have no feeling from the knees down to my toes. I have to wear braces to make sure they hold me up. Being in bed so long has slackened the muscles and pinched the nerves. If I want to walk as before, I'll have to put them through daily exercise. But so what! I've decided to meet the press on my own two feet and I'll do it. Without help, without support, all alone!

As soon as I get past the door of my room I can see them at the end of the corridor. They are keeping a respectful distance, waiting. Laboriously I place one foot ahead of the other. I'm moving forward. It's going to be all right; my legs are holding up. For a few seconds the journalists hang back, their attention riveted to each step bringing me gently towards them. Then, suddenly, everything explodes. No, I'm not going to crumble under the hail of flashbulbs. I continue to advance slowly towards them into the pool of spotlights, the whir of motors, the clicking of cameras. I'm trembling, hesitant, my steps uncertain. I must stay on my feet! The barrage continues, blinding me. And then suddenly I understand. I feel the incomparable sensation of being the centre of everything, the star. I smile a triumphant smile. I'm certain of being a heroine now. This feeling has nothing to do with what I felt at the press conference three years ago when I revealed my sad verdict; no false humility now. I'm radiant under the beams of the projectors. Today I've come to tell the people

193

of Quebec that they were right to believe in me. I deserved their confidence. I'm here today as proof that I've won. My legs obey me, trembling but moving forward. I'm alive! I can guess the astonishment and incredulity on their faces. I can't see it; I'm blinded, a little befuddled, but still moving.

Yves and Isabelle have been following me, one on each side of the corridor, adjusting their steps to mine. The end is in sight now; I'm almost there. Our walk has lasted only a few minutes, but I'm exhausted. "Quick, a chair, please!"

I'm surrounded by microphones and pumped with questions. This interrogation is another ordeal because my voice is so feeble. It doesn't matter, I'll talk anyway. I'm glad to tell the story of my rebirth. I've got one eye fixed on those little sandwiches over there on that table. They're undoubtedly better than the food I've been getting and I want to taste them. I should have the right today: it's my party, isn't it? Dr. Cooper has done things really well. There he is surrounded by his surgeons and the nurses. All the transplant patients are present.

But the crowds are beginning to tire me. Yves and Isabelle take me back to my room, this time in a wheelchair. I'm incapable of taking a single step. Completely washed out. Still, I go on giving interviews from my bed. I overdo it.

And I will pay dearly for my little excess of talkativeness. For several days I'll be paralysed with fatigue. My stomach will refuse any food so they'll have to start the intravenous again. Anger and protest won't get me anywhere. Dr. Cooper laughs at me.

"It's your punishment," he says. "I told you three journalists...."

"But it wasn't me who...."

Bah! It's no use trying to explain, he wouldn't understand. I suppose I deserve my fate. It's what I'd call the price of glory....

CHAPTER THIRTY-NINE

Outside at Last!

February 1–13, 1986

I've been dreaming of getting outside. Being able to breathe brisk fresh air again and put my new lungs to the test is my next objective. I go on like that, always creating new challenges for myself.

"When you've walked your mile, we'll see," said Dr. Cooper.

"A mile?"

"Yes, thirteen times up and down the corridor. Thirteen and a half."

Thirteen times is a long walk, especially with feet you can't feel and toes like cotton balls. All the same, I do it. I walk my mile with determined little steps, back straight, head up. I do have my support team with me, Yves by no means its least enthusiastic member.

"Thirteen, Diane! You're going to make it. Just one more—no, just a half...."

"Okay. Just a half, but it's going to be the hardest."

I knit my brows and refuse to listen to my body protesting in every joint. Whatever I do, I mustn't think about it, just look straight ahead and keep on going.

"That's it! I've done it! I'm a marathon champion!"

In my head a cheering crowd hoists me aloft in triumph. Cooper comes up.

"Good. You can go in two weeks."

"Go? You mean leave the hospital for good?"

"That's right."

"Wow! Give me time to let that soak in. I'll be able to go outside and walk around a little and visit the apartment I haven't even seen since Yves moved in...all that's great. But leaving here for good, that's another story. What do I do if my lungs stop working? What if I have a heart attack? Are you sure of the mechanism?"

Dr. Cooper casts his protective gaze over me like a craftsman contemplating his latest creation. He doesn't seem worried. He knows my insides by heart, almost as though he'd invented them himself.

"You can stay in Toronto for a while and we'll continue to follow you. You needn't be afraid."

"Afraid?" Yes, I'm afraid. I've been hiding the fact so as not to lose face, but I feel panicky at the thought of being at all far from the hospital. I feel like a little girl going away on holidays all by herself, leaving her parents for the first time. The surgeon seems to know all about the solidity of umbilical cords.

"Start slowly. Begin by taking a walk with Yves."

A walk?

Why not? I said I was dreaming of the caress of wind on my skin and the feel of fresh air swelling my lungs, didn't I? But I forgot that winter is so cold. And that's not surprising, because I haven't seen it in three years. The caress of the wind? More like a whip lash. And the cold nipping my cheeks and the snow soaking my feet.... After fifteen minutes I've had enough and we come in. I'm glad to rediscover the warmth and comfort of my room. Yet even though I'd imagined a much more poetic first walk, I'm already beginning to plan others, because once you've begun to taste the air outside, however cold and sharp it is, it gives you an appetite for more. Ghus knows something about that, breathing in his little gulps of liberty. I'll have to ask him if he was afraid the first time he went out. Freedom for a prisoner is perhaps as vast and terrifying as my experience....

Well, for next time I'll need some footwear more comfortable than my thin running shoes. Yves and I go to several stores before we find the right boots. Overshoes rather than boots, in fact, and not very stylish at that. They're heavy and black but they keep my feet on the ground, no risk of my floating off into the air with these on! After finding them, I am able to drop into our apartment, and then I even spend the night there. Oh, not very courageously, I must admit. I'm afraid the whole time. I can only get to sleep by putting the telephone next to the bed. Fear is a stupid, inexplicable thing. It's a bit like a video clip full of catastrophic little images—you keep running it through your head, unable to stop it. My lungs stop working; the air suddenly gets too thin and won't come into my nose; I seem to be drowning without a drop of water. Yes, it's the fear of death. Incredible, isn't it, after all I've been through? Well, it's probably because I came so close to losing my life that I feel such a need to hang onto it. That month-long black hole in my memory is a little like death, isn't it? And now that I've opened my eyes again, I'm afraid to close them in case the bad dreams return. It'll pass. I know that now. Because fear, too, lets go at the most unexpected moments.

"Feeling better, Diane? That stitch in your side gone? Don't feel pain any more?"

"No, I'm all right, Yves. Keep going, don't stop...."

In case you haven't guessed, Yves and I experience more together than just our arguments. There are times of desire and tenderness too, when body and soul achieve fulfilment. Those are the times I passionately want to rediscover in the intimacy of our apartment. Just a few more hours and I will have left behind the antiseptic atmosphere of the hospital. I'll come back now and then for routine examinations, but I won't feel a prisoner there any more.

My suitcases are ready; I've put on my leather pants and my "heart-lung" sweatshirt with "I left my heart and lungs in Toronto" written on it—a present from Gaétane Bergman, a friend from California. Of course all our friends back there know the news, and I'm very anxious to see them again. It's a great trip to look forward to, another project. My head is buzzing with them. For the time being, the most immediate one is to get through that door. After the customary farewells and the traditional photograph, I'll take my man's arm and I'll walk out of here on my own two feet. Tonight we'll celebrate my release in a little French restaurant called Au Clair de la Lune—a pretty name for a place to have an intimate dinner. The manager will recognize me and present me with a rose. I'll eat well, cheating a little, then we'll come back, Yves and I, to our own apartment. And who knows how the evening will end?

"Are you coming, Diane? Are you ready?"

Yves has a suitcase in each hand.

"Yes, I'm coming."

"Do you remember when you were in intensive care all tied up in tubes and machines and you pointed to the door and told me you wanted us to leave?"

"Almost.... It's quite vague. I think I remember because you've told me about it. For me it's more like a dream."

"Well, this time, Diane, it's true. Your dream is coming true at last."

Maybe, but to me it's as though another one was just beginning....

CHAPTER FORTY

The Courage to Live

March 14–16, 1986

"The fog's too thick. No planes are taking off. All flights from Toronto are cancelled."

"Ones to Quebec too?"

"Everything!"

The airline agent is intransigent. He seems to be upset about it, but no more than me.

"Yves! I promised Simon I'd be in Quebec today.... What are we going to do now?"

Simon Bédard is program director for radio station CJRP. He and Christiane Cantin have followed every step of my adventure and have kept their listeners informed. They collected a lot of money when I was in California and have continually encouraged me. I owe them a great deal beyond accepting this invitation from Simon to come and celebrate the success of my operation. He is expecting me and has organized a series of interviews. It's impossible to back out at a few hours' notice.

"We'll take the bus, Diane."

But as it happens, the buses are full. It's always possible to go by car but I suspect Yves doesn't feel much like driving the 800 kilometres. Me neither. The last time we drove to Montreal I was scared to death. Yves had insisted, thinking that this little trip would do me good and get rid of some of my hang-ups. Yes, I was still afraid my lungs would stop working and there'd be no one there to look after me. To make matters worse, it began to snow half-way there, cutting us off from the rest of the world like inhabitants of the Antarctic. Winter is fine, but it's pretty frightening on an icy freeway with snow sticking to the windshield and blocking out visibility. "Can you see all right? Have you got enough gas?" What if we had a breakdown, with not a house in sight? It must be terrible to die of cold...! But I finally managed to talk myself around. I'd had enough of being afraid to die, and besides, it wasn't like me to be a scaredy cat. I told myself it wasn't worth going through the ordeal of a transplant just to be reborn with the mentality of a wimp. I was beginning to understand that the fear that gripped me was not the fear of dying but the fear of living. I relaxed and watched the snow fall, trying to think of nothing. That made the storm seem magnificent and the journey not so long. But to begin all over again with this fog....

"What about taking the train?"

"That's an idea. We could sleep on the way. You'd be less tired when we got there. I hope we can still get a reservation."

Yes, they'd added a few cars and we got two berths one above the other. It's fun to go by train when you've only taken it once before in your life as a very small child. It's restful too, and in no time I'm asleep, lulled by the purring of the wheels. I sleep like a log and wake up in great shape for the change of trains in Montreal.

A few hours more and it's another fairytale adventure in Quebec. Simon Bédard has spared no pains. Brunch with him and a host of friends, then a police escort to a shopping centre where Madame the Mayor of Ste-Foy and a crowd of enthusiastic admirers are waiting for me. I'm caught up in the whirlwind of radio and TV interviews and receptions. Yves's family and mine are also there for the party and are generously invited to an exquisite dinner offered by Monsieur Terzini at his restaurant, Le Café de la Paix. In the evening there's an ovation for me at the Colisée, where we watch a hockey game between Minnesota and Quebec. Have I already said I don't like the play-offs? I'm ready to eat my words. It's much more impressive to be sitting behind a benchful of hefty players than to watch them skating on the TV screen. I don't like being passive; in general I'd much rather play than watch. But I suppose my lousy physical condition will keep me in the ranks of the spectators for some time. Anyway, I have to admit the Stasnys skate faster than I do.

After a night in the Château Frontenac, more receptions, one of them given by the Lieutenant-Governor and his wife. I'm not used to such high society. Despite the superb fur coat CJRP presented me with yesterday, I feel a little out of place in the midst of all the glitter. But everywhere I find the same simplicity and the same admiration for my courage.

All of this might have gone straight to my head if I hadn't taken advantage of this visit to Quebec to meet Nancy Desharnais. This young woman is suffering from an illness very like pulmonary hypertension, and according to her doctors she should have a transplant. She won't have to leave the province, however, because Montreal now has a program like the one in Toronto. Nancy is very young—only twenty-two—and seems very glad to see me in flesh and blood. I suppose meeting me will reassure her and build up her hopes, because this operation still remains very mysterious for most. Indeed, some people talk of my rebirth as though it were a real resurrection. Even Dr. Cooper dropped the word "miracle" speaking about the happy outcome of my five operations. And I'm far from denying my own faith or underestimating the possibility of divine intervention. On the contrary, I think my "Big Pal in the sky" must have given a real boost to my doctors and my own subconscious.

But I didn't spend two years waiting in California for a heart and a pair of lungs without realizing that something must be done about the shortage of donors. Everyone can contribute to prolonging the life of a fellow human being. From a practical point of view, transplant operations are just a kind of recycling. People should get over their fear of having their bodies reused rather than buried in the ground. They should realize the importance of signing their organ donor card—it's a way of participating in the great cycle of life. I've always been preoccupied by thoughts like these, and I've never ceased promoting the cause. Now that I've triumphed in my fight against death, I've become the living proof of what I stood up for. People listen to me with real fervour, and I sometimes have the impression, when I'm speaking into a microphone or before an audience, that they're hanging on my words. I feel they're ready to follow me.

In the plane on the way back to Toronto, I mull over these thoughts excitedly. As for Yves, he's exhausted. He doesn't feel like talking.

"It's fantastic, Yves, I wasn't even afraid when the plane took off. I think I'm cured of my panic. It's as though a new life were beginning for me. When we come back to Montreal they want to throw a big party for me like the one we just had. It'll be fun, eh?"

"For you, maybe.... You know, an artist's life is tiring when he's not the star. I'm just the prince consort."

"It's true I was treated like a princess."

"Absolutely. I heard people behind us whispering that you looked like Lady Diana."

"What? Oh, that must have been because of the hat. Christiane told me it was very chic. I didn't think it was that impressive. But I don't want to be like anyone else, even a princess. I just want to be myself, Diane Hébert!"

"It seems to me you're beginning to play the star."

"Not at all! You're jealous...."

"No, but I find they're laying it on a bit thick...your patience...your courage...."

"So what? I was courageous!"

"Yes, but not any more. You get into a flap over nothing."

"Don't worry, it's almost over. It's just memories, little left-over shreds of nightmares. In a few more days I'll be just like you."

"Like me?"

"Yes, like everyone else, neither more nor less courageous than anyone, but with the will to win."

"Win? Win what?"

"..."

"I know you, Diane, you're cooking something up."

"Do you think so?"

CHAPTER FORTY-ONE

Every Day a Celebration

May 15, 1986

This book could stop anywhere now. My life is going along pretty well like that of any young woman of twenty-nine who has just moved again.

"Be careful, Diane, don't get too tired. Don't lift that box, it's too heavy for you, leave it, I'll take it."

"Go on, Yves, I can do it!"

Now my man has to get me to put the brakes on. If I had my way I'd be working from morning till night. I want everything to be just so in this modest five-room apartment we've moved into. I want Isabelle's room to be especially pretty and welcoming. For the time being my daughter is just coming on weekends, but I hope she'll be living with us permanently. It won't be easy, because her father refuses to turn her over to me. He claims the state of my health won't permit me to look after her full-time. But what does he know? He can't see how active I am. I've turned into a regular little housewife.

It hasn't been all that long, though. Even in Toronto I was picking up on my activities little by little—lots of visits with friends, and a wonderful little party given by Normand and Chantal Côté to celebrate my departure. And the first few weeks back in Montreal were weeks lived in the public eye: radio and TV interviews, press conferences, galas and exhibitions, hockey games, talks—I was everywhere at once. I even went dancing, as I'd promised I would. For a month I had no time to myself; I didn't know where to give my head or my heart. I discovered the fleeting pleasures of popularity. I was spoiled: I received a car and magnificent presents, I was elected "Minister of the Future" by the Salon de la Femme, I was awarded a trophy as one of the ten women of the year. I admit that all these advantages had a certain value in my eyes as recompense for my incessant efforts to stay alive. And yet if I agreed to come back home in such a public way it was above all to thank people, near and far, who had participated in the success of my operation: I wanted to thank them for their support and acknowledge their generosity, and I also wanted to make another appeal to them. Yes, I had one more little favour to ask them. But I had no idea they would respond so rapidly.

One more favour, because others like me who are afflicted with serious illnesses that require transplants are still far from assured of having a successful operation. Even if Dr. Guerraty of the Royal Victoria Hospital in Montreal has set up a program like the one in Toronto, even if he is just as far ahead as his colleagues in California or Toronto, he too is bound to run head on into the scarcity of donors. As I write, four people are waiting in Montreal for an operation like mine—and their chances of remaining alive depend on the same factor. Doctors can only procure organs from people who have given their consent. Right now the organ donor consent form only appears on drivers' licences, which deprives us of a great many donors.

In my interviews and public appearances I never failed to ask for public support in Quebec to change this state of affairs. It seems to me that the consent form should appear on the Medicare card. I started the ball rolling to make this change and circulated petitions. I never doubted that I'd win this battle too, but didn't know what a short time it would take.

This morning a journalist phoned me with the news: the government has agreed, we will now be able to give consent on our health insurance cards. The Minister of Health and Welfare didn't wait for my visit or the numerous petitions that had been signed. I must admit I was caught a little off guard. For a few minutes I felt let down, as if someone had stolen my project.... Okay, what am I going to do now? But I won't have far to look. I know there is a huge amount of work left to do in raising public awareness.

I understand the reluctance people feel about organ retrieval. Some fear they will suffer after death. Yet they should understand that there is no feeling after death. In case they are still in doubt, I hasten to point out that doctors remove these organs with infinite respect for the donor, and only after they are certain of cerebral death. As for those who fear mutilation, they only have to think of what happens to their bodies after death. For my part I prefer the thought of gloved surgical hands a thousand times over that of reprehensible little beasties that live underground. I'm sure the heart and lungs in my breast at this moment would be in an advanced state of decomposition if the thirty-four-year-old woman who had them before me hadn't put her signature on a little card. Yes, that's all I know about my donor, but I think about her often because I know she is living in me. If she hadn't made me this posthumous gift, I'd be dead. It's a fact, the doctors told me I wouldn't have lived past Christmas. And she would have been dead anyway. For *nothing!*

And yet this simple gesture didn't cost her anything. It's a gift of love she made me—and also those who received her liver, her kidneys, and her eyes. No, I'm wrong—it's much more than a gift, it's a heritage she has willed us. This young woman made her will and left us her most precious possession, her life. Yet there are still people who believe that wills are pieces of paper that put their lives in danger....

I realize I won't be able to convince everyone. This question of life and death related to transplants only concerns a small fraction of humanity. Not many people on this planet are victims of pulmonary hypertension. It's something that happens to others, isn't it? I certainly never imagined that one day I'd be afflicted with such a rare disease. And yet it happened—and I think that even if my state of health had necessitated a more common kind of transplant, I would be just as concerned over these questions.

If I have chosen to tell my story in detail, it's not to ensure my popularity or to indulge myself by putting my conjugal problems down on paper. Yves played such a primary role and shared my experience so closely that I couldn't pass over our little conflicts in silence. I've tried to make this book tell as faithfully as possible all the events that took place during this period. We lived them very simply; we're just ordinary heroes. Maybe that's what I wanted to show most. On the other hand, our experience wasn't exactly commonplace, and it taught us a good many things about human values, about trust, about solidarity and friendship.

If this book can help those who are waiting for a transplant, so much the better. I hope I haven't frightened them in describing the interminable waiting or the details of my own setbacks; it goes without saying that not every patient encounters the same difficulties. At Stanford I witnessed very short waiting periods and rapid recoveries; there were as many different scenarios as there were cases. Mine lasted three years, and I'd like to be able to say that it ends here. Yes, I'd like to, but who knows? I'm far from believing that my transplant is a life insurance policy. I'm very much aware that a new reprieve has been granted me, and a new countdown has begun. This time I have absolutely no idea how long it will last. In this sense I'm the same as everyone else: I don't know how or when I'll die.

If I've chosen to end my book today, it's not just because of my little victory. This afternoon I had news from Stanford. As usual it was good and bad. First the good: since I left five recipients have had their hopes fulfilled. Last week Howard, our friend and fellow tenant, had his chance. He had to wait as long as I did. Unfortunately, I also learned that Judy Skidmore, another companion of those first meetings, had waited in vain. She died on May 6, the same day as Stanford's number one, Mary Gohlke, the journalist whose interview I published in *The Gift of Life*. She had survived five years.

Five years. Perhaps that's the time I've got left. Only five years? Maybe more, maybe less.... What difference does it make, though, because I live from day to day and cherish every instant. I can go up and down stairs now and walk without getting out of breath. I can cook, do the housework, go shopping without having to count on anyone. I can do nearly everything all by myself, and it's a pleasure I don't deprive myself of, one I rediscover every day and savour in greedy little sips.

Before I left Toronto I accompanied my friends in the choir of the Church of the Sacred Heart one last time. It goes without saying I couldn't sing. According to the experts it's very unlikely I'll ever recuperate the voice I had before. It's not the least of my disappointments, for I'd have liked to praise my "Big Pal in the Sky" in my own way. But if he doesn't want it that way, so be it. I'll thank him differently. For that matter I rather like this new voice, a little hoarse and a little muffled, just as I like my brown hair and my hard nails. My features have changed and that leads me to believe that my character may have undergone some changes too.

But nothing is less certain. I'd like to be able to say I'm not the same person. It's not true. If I had really changed I would doubtless be satisfied to stay at home and look after the house. But I'm still actively involved in my awareness-raising campaign. It's a kind of mission I've given myself. But I did spend today with my nose buried in my pots and pans. Too bad if my tomato sauce isn't as good as Yves's; when he gets back from work today, supper will be ready. All he'll have to do is sit down at the table. Today we've got something to celebrate. No, it's not my little victory or the successes of Stanford. In fact it isn't an extraordinary event of any kind. I just want to celebrate this day as if it might be the last. I want to relish every minute of it because I know how much each one is worth.

CHAPTER FORTY-TWO

Today

June 22, 1988

I finished writing this book more than two years ago and, as I promised myself, I've lived each day since to the full. The miracle renews itself for me every morning: even before I open my eyes I know that today will be beautiful, unique. I contemplate it in advance, full of inexhaustible wonder. I want to take it in slowly, savouring each sip, like drinking down a big glass of fresh water.

But besides these happy awakenings there have been, I must admit, other more difficult mornings when I feared I was going to lose everything so hardly won. Yes, sometimes I've been afraid. In February 1987 I was hospitalized for a month; a simple bout of pneumonia suddenly degenerated into bronchiolitis obliterans, a dangerous infection well known to people who have had heart-lung transplants; several of my Californian friends died of it. Once again, however, I was lucky; my left lung was damaged but remained active, although it's now particularly susceptible to cold.

That was the first serious trouble I had had after my operation, and it served to slow me down a little. I have to confess that in my eagerness to become my old self again I had often pushed my body to the limit. In the summer of 1986 I had played a lot of sports, even baseball, and I could run for miles without feeling tired. That winter I had continued to force myself, testing my strength and endurance. I think I needed the challenge; I would never have been satisfied to end up doing less than I was capable of before my illness. It was a sort of game, as though I were set on making up all the time I'd lost sitting around trying to catch my breath.

Nowadays, I think I've grown a little wiser. I don't need to burn up my supply of energy quite so fast; on the contrary, I've been trying to channel my reserves to make the efficient use of them. That doesn't mean I'm inactive. I'm always busy around the house with various chores and keep on experimenting in the kitchen, with results that Yves seems to appreciate. But in my spare time, rather than take violent exercise, I prefer to do something useful.

When my book came out in French, I had the opportunity to travel around Quebec promoting it, giving talks and interviews. This allowed me to see how interested people all over the province were in the cause of organ donations. The death of Nancy Desharnais, as well as those of several people waiting for organ transplants, made the shortage of donors even more flagrant. Although more and more people are deciding to make a gift of their organs, some of them forget to sign their donor cards. Others neglect to tell their families about their decision, and the posthumous gift they intend remains ungiven because the reluctant next of kin are too slow to sign a release.

For time is of the essence. As soon as a potential donor has been identified, the medical team should be able to obtain the family's consent, without further delay. Together with some close friends I have formed a committee to draw up and lobby for legislation to speed up this procedure, similar to legislation that already exists in several American states. Such a measure would not only increase the number of operations possible but also reduce the length of time people have to wait for transplants and grafts.

I am spending a lot of time with people who have medical problems that require this type of operation. I visit them in clinics and hospitals and try to encourage them. I've also started up a project to help them get through the waiting period. The Diane Hébert Foundation was incorporated in November 1987 to provide future transplant patients with direct assistance, monthly meetings, and a newsletter. Plans are now being made for a reception centre furnished with the latest medical equipment for patients who come from outside Montreal.

On March 31 of 1988 there were 326 people in Quebec waiting for transplants and grafts of various kinds. The following table shows the steady growth in this type of operation since 1982. The success rate has now reached 80 per cent and is clearly linked to recent developments in anti-rejection drugs. The Foundation will allocate part of its funds to research in this area.

Because of the damage to my lung, I had to join my parents in Florida for the winter of 1987–88. Yves came down and stayed with us on his holidays. He used to detest fishing, but now he's let himself be won over by the quiet charms of the sport. I like to watch him bent over the grey water, absorbed and motionless, his profile a little blurred in the morning mist. He's changed. He seems more serious now, more thoughtful...maybe a little older.

For a few moments I entertain this thought, which makes some people fearful. Looking at him, I tell myself, "Yves is getting older. I'm getting older. We're both getting older together." And I take a deep breath of the tangy ocean air. I sniff it, suck it in, absorb it, hold it, and swallow in all I can of this moment's happiness.

Organ Transplants in Canada in 1987

Organ	Transplants Performed	Patients Waiting
Heart	131	51
Lung (single)	6	5
Lung (double)	6	2
Heart & Lungs	7	17
Liver	102	23
Kidney	733	1,143
Pancreas	6	—
Cornea	1,956	922

"Patients Waiting" includes only those on an active waiting list as of Dec. 31, 1987. Note that figure for kidney transplants does not include transplants from living relatives; also that figure for pancreas transplants includes some combined kidney and pancreas transplants. Figures supplied by Health and Welfare Canada.